BEST *of*
AUSTRALIAN
POEMS
2024

ACKNOWLEDGEMENT
OF COUNTRY

Australian Poetry is based in Naarm, Melbourne, working in offices and remotely on both Wurundjeri Woi Wurrung and Boon Wurrung lands.
We acknowledge their Elders, past and present. As a national poetry body, we also acknowledge that we work across many lands and communities, and we extend our deep respect to all First Peoples, not just in Australia, but across the globe, including poets and audiences, and their enduring connection to Country.

Best of Australian Poems
SERIES PUBLISHER
Australian Poetry

BEST *of* AUSTRALIAN POEMS 2024

GUEST EDITORS

KATE LILLEY

&

SHASTRA DEO

First published 2024 by
Australian Poetry
www.australianpoetry.org

This book is copyright. Aside from fair dealing for the purposes of study, research, criticism, review, or as otherwise permitted under the Copyright Act, no part may be reproduced by any process without written permission. Inquiries should be addressed to the publisher. Individual poem's copyright retained by the authors.

National Library of Australia
Cataloguing-in-Publication data:
Best of Australian Poems 2024
ISBN: 978-0-9923189-5-6

Publisher: Australian Poetry / australianpoetry.org
Guest Editors: Shastra Deo, Kate Lilley
AP Publisher / Commissioning Editor: Jacinta Le Plastrier
Editorial Associate / Social Media Communications: Jennifer Nguyen
Production / editorial assistance: Angela Martinkus
Designer and Typesetter: Chris Edwards
Cover Artwork: Sophie Gaur
Printer: Lightning Source

Publisher's Note

It is AP's policy as publisher across all our publications to remain independent from the selection of poems and editorial commentary made by our guest editors, whose autonomy and curatorial independence we fiercely respect. First Nations Cultural Protocols are also strictly followed, as directed by AP's First Nations Cultural Protocols Director, Yvette Henry Holt. Separately to this, any use of another person's work by contributors is expected to be acknowledged in notes, and the responsibility for this, along with biographies supplied, remains with the poets. We also respect spelling and grammatical variations of poets. New guest editors are appointed for all publications and the themes of publications are finalised and commissioned 12–18 months ahead of each, as required by funding timelines. AP takes its responsibilities to provide methods of excellence and support, and assiduous editorial production processes extremely seriously with very high, proven skill sets among those who work on our projects; this includes offering our duty of care to guest editors, other editors, all contributors, editorial, design and production associates, readers and audiences, and staff. Poetry is a language for life, a trued and compassionate, also exploratory and experimental, language of essence, which has provided meaning for all communities across millennia.

Support

AP would like to thank all publishers, platforms and other organisations that support the flourishing of Australian poetry. We particularly thank our core funders for supporting this publication, which has been assisted by the Australian Government through Creative Australia, its arts funding and advisory body. We also thank a number of generous, private patrons.

Foreword

We acknowledge the traditional owners of the lands on which editing and publishing *Best of Australian Poems 2024* took place: the Boon Wurrung, Wurundjeri Woi Wurrung, Turrbal and Jaegera, and the Gadigal of the Eora Nation. The poems collected here were written across many First Nations lands. Although colonial violence continues to this day, Aboriginal and Torres Strait Islander peoples have a long and unbroken history of storytelling that is essential to Australian poetry. Always was, always will be Aboriginal land. As Jeanine Leane writes in '2020 Vision':

> … there's a war on, what else do you call it? Blak people
> dying in police cells, women still not being heard,
> girls still being raped, young Blakfellas 26 times more
> likely to end up in jail than whitefellas,
> they still take our children over and over and over …

> … I was born on stolen land, my children born
> on stolen land, there's a pandemic in this country,
> began in 1788, no vaccine in 2020 – only resistance,
> wake up every day stronger than all our traumas
> again and again and again …

2024 marks the fourth iteration of Australian Poetry's *Best of Australian Poems*. Creating a poetic snapshot of the year past, this anthology collects works written or published between July 2023 and August 2024. In keeping with the 2021, 2022, and 2023 anthologies, guest-edited by Ellen van Neerven and Toby Fitch, Jeanine Leane and Judith Beveridge, and Gig Ryan and Panda Wong respectively, we have collected 100 poems that intrigued us, surprised us, rallied us, took the tops of our heads off. We thank past editors—as well as *Best of Australian Poems*' predecessor, Black Inc.'s *The Best Australian Poems* (2003–2017)—for the range of vibrant and vital perspectives represented in previous anthologies and are grateful for the opportunity to continue this dialogue with poets and readers alike.

Rather than decreeing the "best" poems of the year—an impossible task—we hope *Best of Australian Poems 2024* is instead the best way to encounter the breadth, complexity, and originality that Australian poetry has to offer. Poems were chosen from the thousands, with the majority selected from the open callout for published and unpublished works. Alongside submissions, we read across print and online collections, chapbooks, journals, and magazines, supported by Australian Poetry's editorial team in seeking out ephemeral performances and projects that exemplified the richness and variety of poetry. Following the example of *Best of Australian Poems 2023*, we also took the opportunity to publish static iterations of digital poetry—a keen reminder that poems are consistently iteratively, reconfigured in the space-time of their reading, digital or otherwise.

Best of Australian Poems 2024 would not exist without the work of Australian Poetry, including Jennifer Nguyen, Jacinta Le Plastrier, Chris Edwards, and Sophie Gaur. Thank you for your trust, diligence, and hours on hours of support, reading, typesetting, retypesetting, and the unquantifiable labour you have put into this anthology. We are also grateful to the Wheeler Centre for their ongoing partnership with Australian Poetry—many thanks for generously hosting the launch of *Best of Australian Poems 2024* in early 2025. We also thank all the publishers and organisations that originally published many of the poems in this anthology, and the publishing houses, small presses, journals, magazines and zinemakers that form the rich ecology of poetry publishing in Australia. Finally, we thank all the poets who contributed to the Australian poetry landscape this year, whether through writing, reading, criticism, or conversation. We appreciated the opportunity to read and learn from your work and would have liked to include many more poems and poets—but that is the nature of editing. The intentions and accidents behind the act of curation are always interesting. As in previous years, the poems in this anthology are organised alphabetically by title—we hope you find resonances in their ordering. We hope you are challenged, inspired and galvanised as you encounter these 100 poems by 101 poets, drawn from many different places, traditions and venues, and that you consider it a lively, partial map of the present state of 'Australian poetry', as written or published across the span of a year: a 'centocartography', to borrow Dave Drayton's excellent coinage. Each poem is singular in its intricacy and specificity while also resonating in innumerable ways with the contents of the volume as a whole, the texts and people and events alluded to, and the lives of readers.

Bringing well-known and emergent voices together, our selection reflects our own preferences and allegiances, as well as our desire to do justice to the lively heterogeneity of the current scene. Here are self-contained poems and poems excerpted from much larger projects, expansive and minimalist lyrics, prose poems, set forms, visual experiments, epistolary addresses, intertextual erasures and recombinations, translations and mistranslations, ekphrases, elegies, lullabies, pastorals and much else. The voices and modes are sincere, ironic, imagist, surrealist, processual, narrative, personal, impersonal, collagist, expressivist, citational, witty, arcane and demotic. As befits a dual-edited, panoramic project of this kind, the strategies of poesis, of composition and decomposition, do not always 'agree' or sit easily together, but all of them are 'high on language' (Pam Brown's phrase). Together they give a strong sense of the stakes of Australian poetry at the present time, in all its dazzling g/local variety, its commitments and engagements, its moods and memes. Fortuitously, the anthology's alpha-by-title sequence closes with Andy Jackson's 'You Speak Clouds', its final enjambed sentence: 'asked what's on/ your mind, you open up your arms to say, *this, all of this*'. As Rory Green writes, 'If there is still a future then we are a part of it.' Poetry in Australia has a future and this is part of it. Now, over to you. We wish you as much pleasure and interest in reading as we have had in selecting them for you, and many further lines of flight.

—*Kate Lilley & Shastra Deo*

Contents

DAMEN O'BRIEN	3	123 Metres
JEANINE LEANE	4	2020 Vision
CATHERINE VIDLER	6	abc poem
GIG RYAN	7	Acrobatics
NADIA RHOOK	8	after the borders open I'm flying to home with poems
GABRIEL CURTIN	10	After the Public Reading
KATHRYN CROWCROFT	15	After the Wedding
HAROLD LEGASPI	16	Ammobium Alatum and Myosotis (Everlasting and Forget-Me-Nots)
KEN BOLTON	17	And John, a Note to You
A.J. CARRUTHERS	20	Antic Cinquains 30
DAMIEN BECKER	21	Atrophy
MICHELLE D'SOUZA	22	Birthday Letter
LULU HOUDINI	24	Black Box and the Erasing World October 2023
CLAIRE POTTER	25	Black Market
OMAR SAKR	27	Bluey in the genocide
MUNIRA TABASSUM AHMED	28	The Boy Who Turned Into Butter
JAKE GOETZ	30	By a drowned valley estuary: three tracings
ANDERS VILLANI	34	Calm Voice
JOANNE BURNS	37	cataloggia
GEORGIA KARTAS & MADISON GRIFFITHS	38	from *Causality*
DAVE DRAYTON	40	Centocartography: Heathcote
AIDAN COLEMAN	52	Correspondence is
JO GARDINER	53	A Country Childhood
JUDITH BEVERIDGE	55	Dead Possum
L K HOLT	56	Describe the Singularity in the Style of Emily Dickinson
BARNABY SMITH	57	direct poem
ROSLYN ORLANDO	58	from *Ekhō*
ANNE WALSH	60	Elk on the Roof
JULIE MANNING	62	Evening on the River
HANNAH JENKINS	63	forest void
LIAM FERNEY	66	Friends, Romans, neither
THABANI TSHUMA	67	Have you eaten?
CLAIRE MIRANDA ROBERTS	71	White Hibiscus

ANN VICKERY	72	Home ward bound
BENJAMIN DODDS	74	Homophobic Horses
JOSIE/JOCELYN SUZANNE	75	House Clearing as black hole
GRACE YEE	76	how to launch a poem
SCOTT-PATRICK MITCHELL	78	I try to talk to gay men on first dates about Perth Canyon and Deep Time but they don't care
OUYANG YU	80	If it's the honest truth they want me to say
COREY WAKELING	81	If you translate loaches, you're likely to encounter minnows
PASCALLE BURTON	83	iron filings (after Liliane Lijn's *Solar Cutting*)
GAVIN YUAN GAO	84	Itinerant
PAM BROWN	86	Keep guessing
DEBBIE LIM	90	Keeping the Minotaur
JANAKA MALWATTA	92	Kriegszitterer
LOUIS KLEE	93	Landscape Poets
CHLOE MAYNE	96	larapuna
WILLO DRUMMOND	97	Learning to use a drill at forty-three
EMILIE COLLYER	98	Lateral ambling gait
DUNCAN HOSE	102	Lumpen Aristocrats (Paris)
JESSICA L. WILKINSON	104	Madeleine
TRICIA DEARBORN	106	The magic
ELLA SKILBECK-PORTER	107	The Magician
EILEEN CHONG	108	The Mechanisms of Doorknobs
ANNA JACOBSON	112	Memory Curls
DŽENANA VUCIC	113	My father sits in a room alone
MANISHA ANJALI	116	from *Naag Mountain*
DAVOREN HOWARD	120	Next dénouement, 4th floor on the right
LUOYANG CHEN	121	No Cinematic Act Could Counterfeit
CATH KENNEALLY	122	not a drop
LAURIE DUGGAN	124	A notice
ESTHER OTTAWAY	125	On whether I subscribe to my name
ENDER BAŞKAN	126	our neighbours poem
AMY CRUTCHFIELD	131	Overheated
ANGELA GARDNER	132	A Passage Through
THOM SULLIVAN	133	Phalaris / Perennial
NATHAN CURNOW	134	Please stop talking about ancient Rome
PANDA WONG	135	pork lullaby
JAYE KRANZ	138	Portmanteau
AUTUMN ROYAL	141	Reception Theory or How to Sit in an Office Chair

STUART BARNES	142	The record player
STUART COOKE	144	*from* Repetend ('a novel's a relaxing thought')
TOBY FITCH	146	Reverse Horse Poem
DAVID STAVANGER	148	Review
CATH DRAKE	149	Snow Burial
ALI JANE SMITH	150	Still life in brown
MELINDA BUFTON	151	Surely
SHEY MARQUE	152	Synesthesia through Binoculars (or When I thought I saw the Green Comet but it Was Only a Shooting Star)
ASHLEY HAYWOOD	153	The Tableland Hour
FELICITY PLUNKETT	156	Tender
DAVID PRATER	157	Terminal 1: Aer Lingus
RORY GREEN	159	The time traveler promises it all
JILL JONES	160	Thinking in the Heat Wave About Clothes, Coins, Yearning, Flying Foxes and What I Cannot Escape
KERRY GREER	162	Three Days and Six Years
STEPHANIE POWELL	165	Touch free wash
HAZEL SMITH	166	Unbalancing
CHRIS ANDREWS	169	Under Fang
SARA M SALEH	170	Unholy Verses
ION CORCOS	171	An Urn of Ash & Bees
JEN WEBB	172	Voice of America Shortwave Radio Towers Demolished
ADAM AITKEN	173	Weather
STU HATTON	174	when you get me alone
JINI MAXWELL	176	Where it Lives
CLAIRE GASKIN	178	willing
LUKE FISCHER	179	Without Poetry
K A NELSON	180	Words with Bobby McGee
DAN HOGAN	181	Workarounds
MICHAEL FARRELL	183	Wrong Forest
BETH SPENCER	184	You draw the heart
ANDY JACKSON	185	You Speak Clouds (after Van Dyck)
	189	Notes on Contributors
	203	Guest Editors
	204	Acknowledgements and Publication Details

POEMS

123 Metres | DAMEN O'BRIEN

Last night we watched a documentary about free-divers,
filmed as they drifted down into the darkening ocean
with only a rope for company. Some fail to make it back.
The urge to breathe becomes implacable as the surface nears.
That far down, divers must have total faith in their preparation.
At the heart of the documentary was a love story between
one intrepid diver and her coach, who waited above the cryptic
surface of the water for a sign. He has brought her gasping
from the blue lips of death three times before with a kiss,
faithful that she was capable of anything. The necessary trick
of free diving – to believe despite the fist of instinct squeezing
in our lungs. When the last diver seemed disoriented, fumbling
the rope, my wife had to remind me to take a sympathetic
breath and let these quicksilver bubbles rush into the future.
Whatever will happen has already happened, either the diver's
husband will revive her once again or he will not. Above, in the
world of oxygen, her crew hope to confirm the world record
attempt and haul her dripping out of uncertainty. My wife leant
against my chest, resting her head on my shoulder. I wonder if
we aren't both of us engaged in our own world record attempt,
holding on with stubborn faith, pulling ourselves arm over arm
up the guide rope, knowing we must never take a breath.

2020 Vision | JEANINE LEANE

… I was born on stolen land, my Grandmother's Mother
raped, my Grandmother too, my Aunties and my Mother,
I am a link in a bigger chain, I am not told what happened
in 1861, or 1887, or 1907, or 1924, or 1961, I don't need to be
I just live it …

… I am seven generations after Invasion, first
in my family to graduate from high school, my Father's
addicted to grog, my Mother to delusion, I made it through
my teenage years, I should have been right but
I still need something to get me through the night …

… I'm not cured, not even close, I am recovering,
I still smoke more than I should, but I gave up
drinking five years ago, one day at a time,
I still laugh, I still feel, I'm not a victim
I'm a survivor …

… there is no theory for Blak trauma
just sheer blunt force, hit, cut, tear, smash, break
if there are any pieces left you pick em up,
mend em, stick em back together again, go on,
no time to sit down afterwards and write a book …

… our good news never makes it to the radio, or
TV, or newspapers, or the classroom, or the office
or the street, or the bus, or the tram, or the train
we have victories, every day is a victory,
we are still here …

… they tell us there's a pandemic on, people are getting
sick, people are losing their jobs, their homes, their
lives, when they say *people* they mean *white people*,
we're still treated like flora and fauna –
people in name only …

… there's a war on, what else do you call it ? Blak people
dying in police cells, women still not being heard,
girls still being raped, young Blakfellas 26 times more
likely to end up in jail than whitefellas,
they still take our children over and over and over …

… I was born on stolen land, my children born
on stolen land, there's a pandemic in this country,
began in 1788, no vaccine in 2020 – only resistance,
wake up every day stronger than all our traumas
again and again and again …

abc poem | CATHERINE VIDLER

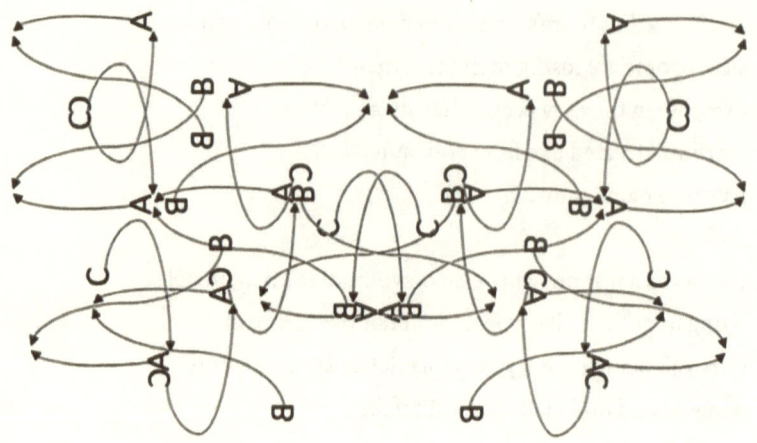

Acrobatics | GIG RYAN

You're not alone in finding it hard to shunt
what matters,
a vogued possum on wire
renounces opulence for aesthetics.
Cars mow night,
his hair quills, wake up to yourself mate,
new wrench same as the old tailspin.

The Treasurer caulked by roses
backpedals from a poll, hoisting marvels,
and departs, a stretched toddler.
Novels end where marriage ends life,
reached out in a tweet.
Yours, prophylactically.

The personal essay drowns in its well.
Now the slightest disagreement's a turnip.
Huffy romantic reads wraparound banalia.
Don't chat to strangers you'll only leave
that atrium that circus that rictus.

after the borders open I'm flying to home with poems | NADIA RHOOK

home (v.) Meaning "be guided to a destination by
radio signals, etc." (of missiles, aircraft, etc.) is from 1920.[1]

… the strange and brutal kingdom
we call home

—ALI WHITELOCK

the porch door still raucous . on metal tracks .
variegated bushes . guarding . the letterbox . bright leaf-lit conversations between
emerald green . wattle yellow . 80s cassette-
radio deck . on the top . of
the fridge. for playing the Hokey Pokey . before school . *yoohoooo* I'm
calling out . to home (caretaker of the door the leaves the fridge)
I'm back, and I've written some poems about you . but home has different .
topics in mind . the next meal . the next doctor's
appointment . who has cancer who doesn't (yet) have
cancer . and so, with

    poems
    resting . on the curved-leg glass-covered
    table . beside us . home and I are speaking .
    over the top of each other . volume . intensifying . fast .
    a siren . a war's fickle distance . and I'm stepping
    away from home . (because home's telling me I should've titled
    the poem with home's language, not the language of the land) and
    I'm sitting down . on a distressed floral cushion . a body's
    length from home . a truce's reach from
    poems . and home is
    searching . my eyes . asking *why do*
    you look sad when what you've been missing is right here?
    and I'm trying (in home's language) . to explain . *I wrote this poem to*
    say "I missed you when the borders were closed" but
a radio on a fridge on Wadawurrung Country sounds out a kingdom lost and

as something begins to
close . home's hands . so richly veined . I
retreat . back . into the cushion . into the verb of it into
the search . for the
verb of it . into
an old meaning of "receive" . vibrating . alarming . our
drums . our peace . only articulated . in a swift move to
talk about . what's for tea . a barely
detectable re-arrangement of our bones

1. 'Home', *Online Etymology Dictionary*, https://www.etymonline.com/word/home.

After the Public Reading | GABRIEL CURTIN

After the public reading someone approached me to compliment our text and asked if he'd stumbled on a Trotskyist meet-up. *Everyone here seems to know one another, and everyone seems to be a communist, but no one seems to know what kind of communists they are.* I told him I didn't know lots of the people there but that his second observation could be true. I offered a Priyamvada Gopal quote that describes communism as *a common global language in which both the identification of oppressive structures and liberation from them can be articulated.* Then you came over and the two of you started chatting while I drifted off to thumb through the journal that had just launched and have short conversations stilted by goodbyes.

I don't think he minded that people didn't know what kind of communists they were. I didn't either. Marx has that quote about bureaucracy, *its hierarchy is a hierarchy of knowledge.* We felt to be doing what we needed to be doing, together, that afternoon, despite the dispiriting surrounds of a city rejuvenation project. Any lack of obvious allegiances was less a failing of rigour and more a putting aside of acquired knowledges to focus on the task at hand: naming our duress, doing what we want to keep.

I text you about the hat you lent me and the praise it received from strangers all afternoon. You text back and tell me that your Soviet Union soccer jersey had been garnering similar attention from customers at the bookshop where you work. Then: *A guy came and bought Marx, said, "you have to read Karl every few years" then made a shock face when he saw my shirt, asked if it was nostalgic and I said no.* The shock face belongs to your daughter, it is a sudden inhale through a puckered O shaped mouth, eyes wide, eyebrows up, palms shaking beside cheeks. It's the expression of sudden overwhelm, the afterimage of being very alive. We all love it when it appears.

I rode to the State Library this morning and followed closely the rituals you guided me through last week when we came here together. I locked my bike round the corner from the entrance even though I had to ride an extra half block to get there. I peed at the urinal you told me was the one you always use. I filled my water bottle up from the tap next to the bathroom, not the bubbler near the entrance. Making coffee for us the other morning you berated me for doing it uncaringly. I ground more beans than was necessary, didn't stir the water when I added it, pressed the plunger early. You were in an irritable mood but generally it's a trait I appreciate—careful attention to process. You have lots to say on the matter, and I agree that being in the form of the labour is critical, otherwise everything becomes mediated through the product—we even wrote about this in the text the Trotsky-meet-up-person complimented—but I think even you'd admit sometimes you just like things done a certain way. One example I often give of our differences in approach is how I arrive on time but hungry and without anything I need, whereas you arrive late but well fed and with everything everyone might need.

Some people that heard the excerpt we read thought it was about hating work. I found myself replying that it was more about the things we defer when going to work. What I mean by this is that we work to live and, hopefully, eke out what we enjoy when we're not at work. But sometimes what we enjoy—that immaterial, iridescent nudge-up against life, that is always not, and never can be, work—shows up amongst it.

I got stoned last night and some friends put on a basketball game. Intensified by the joint, I found the language everyone was using mystifying. Some had more furiously learnt the lingo of the sport, a lingo that ascends registers depending on the calibre of the fan. It felt arbitrary and excessive: naming moves after they were performed, launching staunch analysis on what a player *always* does and why it is a failing, peppering the game with obscure facts and why those facts matter greatly to this specific match up. The language felt coded, more about establishing the speaker's legitimacy than offering something the group could enjoy together. It also felt mimicked, like how your daughter will warm to the sound of a word and start using it, understanding the general logic of speech and syntax but be disinterested in the word's actual definition. I thought about that Marx quote, the one about hierarchies of knowledge. Aware weed can make an inane situation seem stressful, I focussed on how sport lingo is fun, how it becomes a game, a narrative device, a code you refine the longer you practise it, the more games you watch, the more performances you imbibe.

Earlier I wrote that it didn't matter what kind of communists we were because we were doing what we want to keep. I'm rethinking this. Maybe our talk is sport-lingo. It sounds good and it feels good, but is it ultimately a form of procured pacification? Your daughter's shock face is important, I think, because it's a figure for what we're shooting for—the world unabashed, muscling in, entirely overcoming us—how we catch it at times, try to make it abide.

We generalise, talk about getting together then don't. We read at book launches, congratulate one another over wine, but something feels amiss, nothing electric.

My standard issue daily planner work foisted on me features an inspiring quote at the bottom of each weekday. Weekends, no quote. Whoever produced it either assumed no one would be in to read them on weekends or that penalty rates preclude further motivation. Abraham Lincoln, Marlene Dietrich, Isaac newton, Plato, Arthur Schopenhauer,

Donald Rumsfeld, Maya Angelou and Bob Dylan are among the disembodied authors. Today's quote is from Malcom X. It reads *The future belongs to those who prepare for it today*. Whatever that quote might proffer when encountered on a regular, shit-for-brains workday is substantially altered when a good Marxist reads it. Even still, set on the page amidst hundreds of others, the quotes become hard-to-argue-with generalities. They point more towards the merits of organisational prowess than the reorganisation of social imaginaries.

Anyone invested in either figure would never put Rumsfeld in the company of X. But that's how this works, things are given power in specificity. Once cleaved from it, everything can be repurposed. McCartney sings on a Kanye track whose young fans praise Kanye for platforming an unknown artist. Graeber and Wengrow speculate that some neolithic societies practised different social arrangements seasonally, meaning they were able to access each configuration at a remove, understand these configurations weren't fixed or pre-ordained, were subject and able to change. We, instead, at some point, got stuck, convinced the licence to remix at will is immutable.

One accusation we received after our reading was that we meander too much, draw in disparate info and insist on shooting off instead of consolidating an argument. Maybe they're right, that we don't know what kind of Marxists we are but enjoy the tingly sensation we get from reading things we don't understand. Maybe we're a Malcolm X quote in a workplace planner. But I agree with Mary Rueffle when she says:

I will tell you that if you think I know something or anything, I am just pretending to know as a way to pass the time. Personally I think we should all be in our rooms writing. [...] I like things the size of a pea, I like miniature umbrellas and I like walnuts and I like the part in Hamlet where he says he could live in a nutshell and count himself the king of infinite space (were it not for the fact he had bad dreams).

That's what we do. We write (together) and then we read (together). We watch sports and talk about them in a neat suspension *and* exaggeration of our lives. We make things small so they can move freely. Sure, sometimes into diabolical relations. Other times, something more mysterious. One time your daughter was riding on my back, I was her horse. She wanted me to rear up so I lifted my arms into the air. The angle was odd and she lost her grip, slipped and banged her head on the floor. Another time I lodged a red, translucent piggy bank over one of her woollen doll's heads to make a scuba diver. In both instances her eyes went very wide and her mouth formed an O.

After the Wedding | KATHRYN CROWCROFT

I tell myself I will take a handful only.
Plum, heavy with its load, I press
each lobe between digits, extend one hand
through a fork to the cavity's ferment:
wasps, flies, camouflaged green-tipped clits, incensed
stuck feasting at the plum-crease. Some dead
there, crystallized. Urgent desire to thresh –
dead-head the limbs – the ground,
blood & bone. Underfoot, their skins. Nettles seek
an itch, the air picks up,
high trees not far above the plum, their reach
beginning at the point
from which a human could die if she fell.

I took my fill,
one shoulder hinged to meet the weight,
the day pinking about me. And the penned dog
roared as I passed, walking last night's road
littered with tissue paper hearts,
on the perimeter of the farm. I closed
the door of the car, airtight as a donor's heart,
set the plums down & saw the wind
through its screen, lick into branches & leaves,
thrashing at the cope without sound.

Ammobium Alatum and Myosotis
(Everlasting and Forget-Me-Nots) | HAROLD LEGASPI

Garden beds under the heads of yellow florets
Severed by leaves at its base
Faith is the spirit binding deeds
Dirty laundry and secrets

What is *doing* when we could
Be *going*
A spiral of words and lament
For earth and rotten earth

No perfect order
Of rich life flourishing
Unless winter comes each year
It does not snow in Western Sydney

Yes, it is *not* even
Because the heart is shaped like a fist
All that is left is to stay at home
Buried under a blanket

& pick at a mouse's ear

And John, a Note to You | KEN BOLTON

for John Levy

Dear John, I liked the poem. I've liked
most of them I'm sure. But this one
had something about it
that seemed very unusual. Or 'a first'.

(Actually it can't be. *Can* it?)

It seems much more
surrenderingly emotional.

      #

It occurred to me *The Notifications* could be their group title, these
'note' poems. 'A Note to Ken Bolton',
'A Note to … whoever'

      #

For the last day or so, apart from the intrusions
of real life, I've been ransacking my room
(and searching in the computer), for a photo I had—
of John Forbes turning up at a party. In it, I'm wearing
a tall conical hat (paper). We stand
facing each other.
                    Laurie Duggan, I remember,
called it 'John Forbes meets the leader of the
Tolkien Elf Protection Society'

                something along those lines.

      #

I could probably turn *this*
into a
    'Note' for you.
        May do too. Tho
not on my phone
with its tiny screen.

        The Notification of Everyday Life
in the Era of Late High Capitalism.
I could work that in too. Give it
'a touch of the Walter Benjamins'—and portent, portent, portent.

Shall I go on?

I almost feel like I have 'written the poem'—here, now, at 4 AM,
about four hours before I should really clock on.

(The Arts Industry—beloved phrase)

I could quit here.

Back in the middle 80s when a few of us
established a Writers Centre, a friend of mine
when he came in to our
shared space, and found me there, used like to say
'Morning, Ralph'.
        It was a private joke, a reference I didn't get, tho I
liked the phrase, and liked the humour. *Morning, Neil*, I'd say.
I could add, today
Been here since four.

The photo was from the 70s—my days in
Glebe. The poet John Forbes. A strange meeting
is how it looks in the photo: John a looming presence

his back to the camera—& the space opens out
beyond him, & I greet him from within it
pleased he was there

a moment in my life
that I remember only because of
the picture. In fact I *only* remember the picture.

The feel of it comes back—because I knew that room
well—a long narrow kitchen
with views out over the water, to far away Balmain,
tugs, various water craft, barges laden with timber
& city harbour lights at night—our cheap
furniture. I was twenty-six or seven, he
a year younger.

#

    When I look at this hard
I see there's a square of cardboard taped to the window,
patching some broken glass. There's a Chinese
'glorious workers' type poster.
The round 'louvre' high up is not in fact a louvre
but a wooden place mat, 'Chinese' or 'Japanese'.
The bright lights out the window used to throw light
on some large silos way across the harbour
& they may belong to the Iron Cove bridge (which I think
may by now be gone, or re-built
& with a different name). People—*and* the poem—say
'Balmain', but it is
probably the neighbouring Rozelle.

That jumper I'm wearing—bought from Sportsgirl—
a women's item—faun brown. I wore it for years.

Antic Cinquains 30 | A.J. CARRUTHERS

Let curses strangle outworn Music, and Music strangle Music,
Muśics leaf-to-leaf, wither-leaf: Poetíc
Parting dramatic-music, taller withouten drama
Parted at the threat: noose about the notes
Has wrote part of an operatic.

Poems all-unlike the Music, have never become it
Not one now and never put to Music
Now Music to beat; that rung Poetic victory;
Plodding on outside thy broken pitch;
Pooŕly like the ambits patter.

Poetic Music will prevail never, never without paper
To call a Poetic Music burdens craft
Burdens height in muddled wit
So wit will muddle burdened Music, to languish in our English
Plant English where my English will compost.

I set to August
As Goiswinth sang in sorrow: Music lives
To punish fallen poesy
I strike the keys to regulate the universe; as neither Music will
For lesser quill has trained in type.

I system every Music, as thee stanza
I want ńot thy height,
Poetic all has my need; bŕeath-withouten, will blind the wind
Exactly as I wrote it, not as it would have played.
Poet Venantius Fortunatus: 'the music echoes from the rock exactly
       as it passes from the air.'

30 Dec 23, Yarrh

Atrophy | DAMIEN BECKER

Part I.

This body:
alone
a lone
a loan

Part II.

Rate your pain out of throats. Thread a line of prose up through the brachial vein until you know it by heart. An x-ray reveals a gun in your chest. Choose your bed carefully, noting its proximity to the drain. Eat to avoid becoming a stock image face for charities. (The only treatment for your condition is to take a number and wait. Everything is promising and it's amazing what they can achieve with camel organs and pinholes.) Apply your eyes with light pressure.

When you lose all sense of feeling, consult your dog. Sing your phlegm with blood. Flirt with every surgical instrument that could kill you. Mouth a skipped stitch through the purple bruise of your gown. Gauze your tongue to prevent the spread of inflection. Rebuild yourself with blocks of ice. Find a toilet as the only way back in. Wrap your large intestine around the handle to lock the door. (It is your home for now.)

Signing your name in analogue, you may feel a sharp scratch. Swab your ears for traces of Radiohead. Eye contact with the tea lady overwhelms the smell of tabloids. The physio advises to stay on the treadmill until jelly crystals form. (It is best to keep moving to aid recovery of the food.) Gift ward rounds their mourning rings round the bed like you are already in the hole. Note in your file that everything tastes of balloons.

Ghost the other patients trying to make a living decent. Confess to plasticjesus nailed to an IV pole that you have never prayed a believer. Med students stress you live alone in their final submission.

Birthday Letter | MICHELLE D'SOUZA

I put my hands among the flames. Nothing burns
—Sylvia Plath

sunset dyes the cliffs orange,
                      their reason
is something delicate as a blue wren's song
when i feed the wallabies carrots they clash,
    like acrobats, bouncing off the red earth
soon it will be time to light a fire, cook soup,
kiss the cold wind,
    to spend an hour trying to capture 4G,
as the sad android icon regrets
    'a network change detected'
calmed by ambient light,
               not yet understanding
    this splitting, part decay,   part bloom,
    but here's an emoji, a link, & a password
    to zoom at 7pm EST

spend hours watching wind-slicked flames,
    branches shrivel to marble,   to ash,
    as the violet evening graces
    with cicada empathy,
    shy wood moths in pipe-cleaner trees,
    this is what i do,
collect cloud artefacts,   worth a look,

red-flecked acacias,

       acrylic lichens on a rotting log where
       a fiddler beetle lays her eggs,
crimson sea fig become Plath's little 'hell flames'

rainbow day of their birth 19 years ago—the backwash
      and undertow dragging sand from the dunes,
           where i photo-text,
   our signal erratic as the southern sea

Black Box and the Erasing World
October 2023 | LULU HOUDINI

███████ and ████████ kiss each others
eyelids days apart.

Bombs erupt in ████████
and ████████ never gets to learn the alphabet.

Attempting genocide in ████████ blueprints
attempted homeland genocide in ████████

████████ fell asleep but ████████ didn't
wake up.

████████ unethically voted for ████████.
████████ is the only one who loses.

████████ and ████████ don't support a ceasefire.

████████ left by foot, while ████████
departed on the wind.

████████ writes the story, while ████████
searches for Truth.

Black Market | CLAIRE POTTER

> From a certain point, there is no more turning back.
> That is the point that must be reached.
> —Franz Kafka

It moved. Like something a double agent might stifle.
The wind turned it inside out and blurred it,
nightfall made it louder.

In some way, you were father to it,
chasing it side-to-side like a vagrant fish
in your black coffee,

my mind its solitary jetty.
Last week the weather felt different, almost maternal.
I put a suitcase of seedlings

into your hands
but piece-by-piece, the leaves broke off
and your hands melted away

like a sun and a moon
that were candles.
Earlier, from twenty-five to thirty-two

I followed you in obeisance.
Took a plane from city to city and then
a train underground—

In the shadow-play of cafés, nightcaps,
the heat of summer rain, when lights
turn red, they smell of you.

It comes again, too often. The questions
mired in amber, the palms of electricity, the sharpness,
from a certain point of view, of supposedly

losing it all. No more silver
into the hard green mouth of the well.
No more wishes drawn

from a wish-soaked heaven.
Cold happiness. The company of thieves—the dark-
berried timber, your blue eyes looking

back as I sit on the staircase
and glimpse the pollen-nest we gambled
like dust into the breeze.

Tonight I forge a promise:
When nobody is home, and the bills are
all paid, I will visit.

Bluey in the genocide | OMAR SAKR

We watch the cricket episode,
All laconic drawls and summer
Games, a dedicated pup learning
To play while his father is away.
His name is Rusty, he's a star
At bat. My son laps it up, as do I
Until the end; the scene shifts
And there is the distant dad
In combat fatigues, and I learn
Even in this cartoon world
There is a desert full of dogs
Soldiers and guns, and somewhere
Out of frame, Arabs being put down.

The Boy Who Turned Into Butter | MUNIRA TABASSUM AHMED

1. The boy presents his fallen baby tooth, now soft and spring yellow, pincered between malleable fingers. A loose printed T-shirt now greased to his chest, the boy accidentally carves a chunk from his cheek, though he manages to seal it back before his father turns around. 2. When the father sees his son, glossy under the nearby lamp, he does all the usual things. He swipes his hands over his son's arms and digs at his shoulders, desperate to find a boy beneath the butter. He calls his brother, the butcher, and asks to borrow a walk-in refrigerator. He pushes against the boy's abdomen, expecting skin to push back or, at least, guts to answer. It is all butter. 3. The father moulds his son to be a little taller before entering the refrigerator. 4. Overnight, the boy is startlingly calm. He pinches his left hand every few minutes and feels no pain. 5. The father does not check on the boy. He sits awake, two rooms away with his door firmly shut, unmoving. 6. Hours pass. The boy believes his father is coming to save him, though he is still unsure if he is alive or not. The nightmares have been getting worse but the boy is not afraid of death. His father told him, after his mother died, that 'death cannot be so bad, no one has ever come back!' 7. His father doesn't speak much. He still sits awake, still unmoving. 8. The boy's denial does not dissipate. It is swiftly swallowed by fear. When he runs out of the refrigerator, he leaves fat between the ridges of the seal and misshapen footprints on the linoleum floor. 9. His father catches up to him in the driveway. There is a thread of dawn in the sky and no witnesses. When he reaches to tackle the boy, the concrete is wet with dew and everything must slip to the ground. It is shockingly easy to break a boy made of butter. It is just as easy to put him back together, though his neck is now buffed with fingerprints. I'm sorry. I wanted to stay with you. I didn't know how. 10. If they remain, holding one another, for a while longer, the boy will melt over his father's beating chest.

1. The boy presents his fallen baby tooth, now soft and spring yellow, pincered between malleable fingers. A loose printed T-shirt now greased to his chest, the boy accidentally carves a chunk from his cheek, though he manages to seal it back before his father turns around. 2. When the father sees his son, glossy under the nearby lamp, he does all the usual things. He swipes his hands over his son's arms and digs at his shoulders, desperate to find a boy beneath the butter. He calls his brother, the butcher, and asks to borrow a walk-in refrigerator. He pushes against the boy's abdomen, expecting skin to push back or, at least, guts to answer. It is all butter. 3. The father moulds his son to be a little taller before entering the refrigerator. 4. Overnight, the boy is startlingly calm. He pinches his left hand every few minutes and feels no pain. 5. The father does not check on the boy. He sits awake, two rooms away with his door firmly shut, unmoving. 6. Hours pass. The boy believes his father is coming to save him, though he is still unsure if he is alive or not. The nightmares have been getting worse but the boy is not afraid of death. His father told him, after his mother died, that 'death cannot be so bad, no one has ever come back.' 7. His father doesn't speak much. He still sits awake, still unmoving. 8. The boy's denial does not dissipate. It is swiftly swallowed by fear. When he runs out of the refrigerator, he leaves fat between the ridges of the seal and misshapen footprints on the linoleum floor. 9. His father catches up to him in the driveway. There is a thread of dawn in the sky and no witnesses. When he reaches to tackle the boy, the concrete is wet with dew and everything must slip to the ground. It is shockingly easy to break a boy made of butter. It is just as easy to put him back together, though his neck is now buffed with fingerprints. I'm sorry. I wanted to stay with you. I didn't know how. 10. If they remain, holding one another, for a while longer, the boy will melt over his father's beating chest.

The boy is all tooth and spring, the usual things.
He pinches his left hand and feels no pain.
alive or not his mother cannot come back
The dawn witnesses the boy, wet with dew and beating

By a drowned valley estuary: three tracings | JAKE GOETZ

                in a clouded oaken wash
                      morning cool and olive
        rises with the tide
                      as a coffee makes
       an atlas of the body
                      warming the stomach
     with the tierra y sol
            y rios de Colombia

          WARNING
       DO NOT EXCAVATE
         SHELL – S.M.P.
        HIGH PRESSURE
         OIL PIPELINES

    pumping oil between
                Gore Cove and Clyde
       the airport and Kurnell
Newcastle and Yenangyaung
         where the resource
     naturally rises to earth's surface
                and for which the British
    invaded Myanmar in 1885
taking control of their oil industry
       and establishing the petrol empire
           Burmah Shell

                *

tracing sheoaks

a pebbled path winds

to *Burial Vaults*

an empty mausoleum

cut from sandstone

for Sydney business tycoon

and one time politician

Thomas Holt   a man who built

a Gothic mansion

on the hill above in 1857

on 'one of the most beautiful sites

in the district'   12 acres stocked

with rabbits   alpacas

and other exotics

but upon his death

the land subdivided

and the building bought

by a French order

of Carmelite nuns

who were eventually evicted

for outstanding debts

at which point

the land transformed

into a WWI artillery range

and after the war

the mansion torn down

                        to build houses
                    for returning soldiers
                one of which my opa would rent
                        in the early 60s
                    a fitter and turner
                        programmed as a kid
                    by the fascist jingles
                of the Hitlerjugend
                13 at war's end and just 22
            when he boarded a ship
                    in Bremerhaven
            spent a year working
                the Port Kembla steelworks
            then moved to Newtown
        where he met an Irish Catholic
                recently arrived from Belfast
            via London

                *

            a group of little black cormorants
        sit on a rectangle of land that juts
                into an artificial harbour
                    a pelican glides   throws out its legs
                        wings extended   rocking left to right
                            like a paratrooper bracing to land

     in the DMZ the way culture shapes
   our speak places Martin Sheen in a kayak
    with an AK47 destabilises one's senses
  from the immediacy of the thing
as the pelican crashes down startling the cormorants
  who launch into the water creating wakes
    for mud crabs to assess
   everything endless in its discussion
     as downriver a metal plaque
   almost hidden among sheoaks

       This is Cadigal Wangal Country
       baram, guwagu, barrabugu
       yesterday, today, tomorrow

Calm Voice | ANDERS VILLANI

On a fatherhood weekend, the men drag
a dead manna gum, chained to a ute, into camp.
They're talking innocence. Is it inborn, or clad
layer by layer by behaviour? Around the grey stump
the men start chainsaws and crack beers, open
a phone (there's reception), search *innocence definition*.
Blamelessness. Chastity. Childhood. But also
integrity, which means innocence. The confusion
—that integrity means wholeness too—
heats up when one man says he heard children
arrive with sin. Then two-stroke fumes
drown the twilight bush's scat-and-pepper scents.
They cut it. Some of the men scream, some don't,
when spiders erupt from the warm hollow.

When spiders erupt from the warm hollow
a man tells a story. Halfway down a hill
between three brothers' house and the park where ghosts
shoot up in the centre of the oval
there's a house, double-block, yellow brick.
It's for orphaned and homeless youths. At night
—any night—twenty kids sleep there. No strict
rules can stop it from sounding like a hundred, like
a Slipknot concert. The exiles find new shadows.
The men roll the logs into the last campers' pit.
Twice in the brothers' childhood, the house goes
up in flames. Cops comb its yard for knives. For bits
of evidence because these kids are bad.
They steal one brother's Razor scooter. They're bad.

They steal one brother's Razor scooter. They're bad
thieves—the two younger brothers see them
from their bedroom, tell their older brother, who's had
enough and leads them down. Twigs, kerosene,
and three 18V leaf blowers and it's blazing,
a mountain range whose peaks scratch the dark sky
of gum canopy and dark sky. They sedate him
with words, calm voices, or try, the carers: *why
risk arrest over this?* The man recalls
the woman saying, *I'm speaking in a calm voice.*
Chanting it. A spell. But there are walls
she bruises then, backing inside. Her voice
like the TV cabinet glass he puts
her through. The boy from a good home. Voids her.

What did the boys from a good home lose, shed, void
that day? Not the older brother, but the
ones on the street who summoned him. The boys
who saw a woman valued less than a scooter
at an age when the worth of things was molten
glass for heroes to blow. It's the world,
one man says. This fire's the world and when
the fireworks go off later, it'll be all
our evolution reaching its end point—
bright lights and explosions. Ginger steeps
in cast iron, drugs strike blood, charcoal anoints
a lentil stew, which dissolves the man's story.
Talk moves on. A herd eating sweeter grass.
One man's dog pulls a roo bone from the ash.

One man's dog pulls a roo bone from the ash
and it turns to spiders, which turn to ash
on the younger brother's eyelids, to ash
in the middle brother's memory settling
when the younger brother comes, asks, *Remember
when you led us down the hill to find the kid
who'd thrown a hot dog at me? Remember
kicking his door till he answered, joined
in calling himself what you called him, licked
my shoes?* The middle brother had forgotten
himself back to an innocence the quick
of which is fire, innate combustion.
Around the fire, the men talk skin-to-skin
touch in the early months, so love burns in.

cataloggia | JOANNE BURNS

the aperitivo antipasto
hour slidels into view
there's something in the air
verando   aperolicks
proseccutions   muebles wickeramas —
organic or synthet   why not just
click/collect

raj meets gatsby in the lumen
of a hubble bubble   no unnecessary
toil or trouble   a wicca wonka
spelling bee pollinates in the furnished
suburbs of the blest

from Causality | *GEORGIA KARTAS & MADISON GRIFFITHS*

III. The Empress

you were born
with thick ursine claws

pluck! at the harp
in your full belly
suck! out its holy
savage venom

its spread χλωρός
(*chloros*, green)
an antidote

Centocartography: Heathcote | DAVE DRAYTON

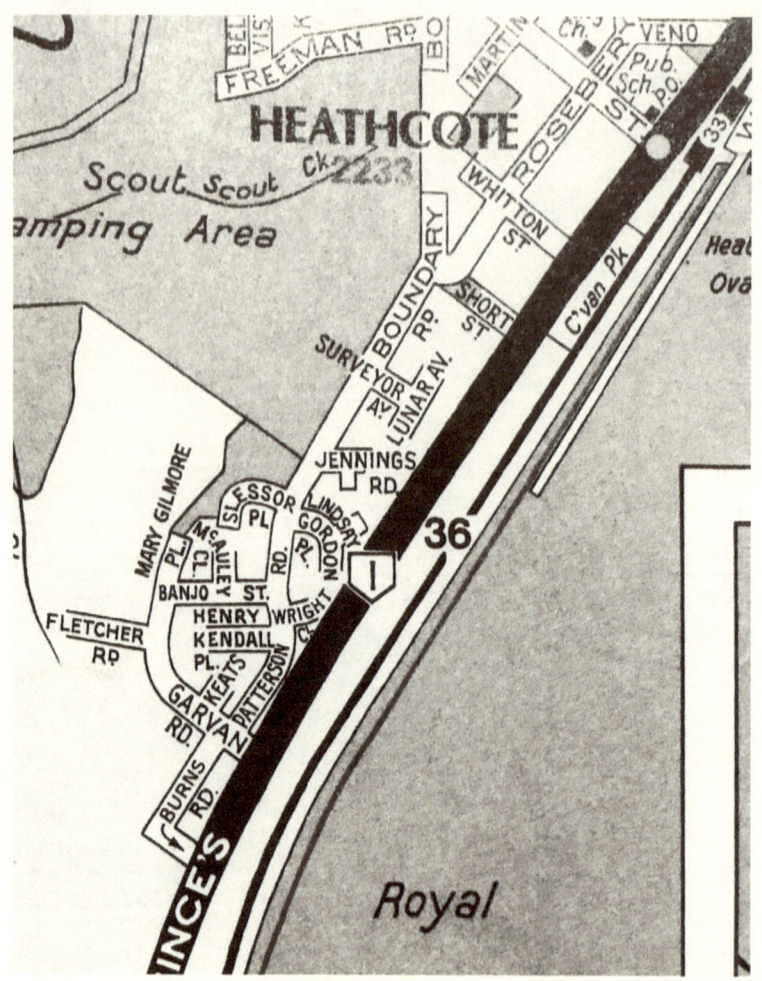

i.

Sometimes she is beauty, sometimes fury, sometimes neither,

To blot them out again. Of white Australia, as she hugely squats And blotted out grief and glory

Australia takes her pen in hand

is not more white and still than she

Will she ever, ever, ever fill this heart?

the national papers the next morning reported that she had someone was desperate to fill in the gaps

Mary Gilmore, 'A Little Ghost'; Kenneth Slessor, 'Polarities'; Adam Lindsay Gordon 'Quare Fatigasti'; Banjo Paterson, 'We're All Australians Now'; James McAuley, 'The True Discovery of Australia'; Henry Kendall, 'Waiting and Wishing'; Judith Wright, 'Late Spring'; joanne burns, 'Australia', joanne burns, 'Australia'

ii.

So men write poems in Australia.

dally—

But I pause, for your fancies poetic

Side by side they

So poetry that moves by chance collision

Whatever poets   and authors   say

Gather into a meaning

With some prolixity of mouth.

cut, planted

their dialects

noise

Mary Gilmore, 'Pejar Creek'; Kenneth Slessor, 'Five Visions Of Captain Cook'; Adam Lindsay Gordon 'Hippodromania; or, whiffs from the pipe'; Banjo Paterson, 'Conroy's Gap'; James McAuley, 'Marginal Note'; Henry Kendall, 'Black Lizzie'; Judith Wright, 'Five Senses'; joanne burns, 'around the traps'; joanne burns, 'noise'

iii.

Has broken, and the ghosts of flesh are stirred

whose steps have passed

Locked in this nameless grave's neglected mound,

You follow us still in your ghostly might

A little ghost

For fear   that his ghost   might walk;

waves of shadow wash

And hither they will flock again, the ghosts of things that are no more,

like some Shakespeare ghost

dead.

Mary Gilmore, 'A Little Ghost'; Kenneth Slessor, 'Realities'; Adam Lindsay Gordon 'Ye Wearie Wayfarer'; Banjo Paterson, 'The Swagman's Rest'; James McAuley, 'At A Child's Grave'; Henry Kendall, 'The Rain Comes Sobbing To The Door'; Judith Wright, 'The Old Prison'; joanne burns, 'moonphrases or/mostly you are invisible', joanne burns, 'bars'

iv.

Would scowl approval, for they were shipmates, too,

They were men for the most part rough and rude

Ashamed to think that Australian men

And whistle like larrikins at you from the trees.

It's grand to be a Western man,

Beside his heavy-shouldered team

Endeavouring daily to destroy

when he smiles, an elbow sharply angled out, tense fist on

of garbage men deconstructing silence;

Mary Gilmore, 'Singapore'; Kenneth Slessor, 'Captain Dobbin'; Adam Lindsay Gordon 'Ye Wearie Wayfarer'; Banjo Paterson, 'It's Grand'; James McAuley, 'Terra Australis'; Henry Kendall, 'A Hyde Park Larrikin'; Judith Wright, 'Bullocky'; joanne burns, 'mere anarchy', joanne burns, 'at home'

v.

Between the sob and clubbing of the gunfire

Anzac!... Tobruk!... and Kokoda!...

Whose field of action is this continent

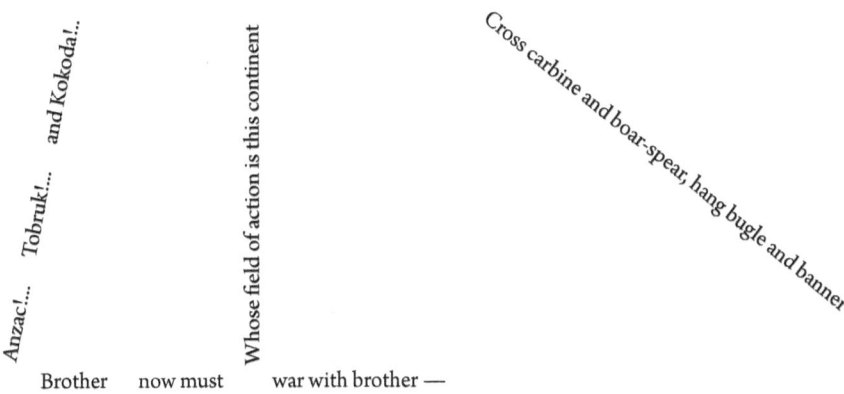
Cross carbine and boar-spear, hang bugle and banner

Brother   now must   war with brother —

Death marshalls up his armies round us now

And say how our brothers were slain,

in a recent anzac
a bullet

Mary Gilmore, 'No Foe Shall Gather Our Harvest'; Kenneth Slessor, 'Beach Burial'; Adam Lindsay Gordon 'The Roll Of The Kettledrum; or, The Lay Of The Last Charger'; Banjo Paterson, 'Ave Caesar'; James McAuley, 'New Jerusalem'; Henry Kendall, 'Urara'; Judith Wright, 'The Company of Lovers'; joanne burns, 'poise', joanne burns, 'elucidations'

vi.

And the world a buried star, not talked about—

As if the world was good,

For the world's bare tokens

Let us run over the world together!"

Whom would it profit?—The world goes round!

We meet and part now over all the world;

The world is round me with its heat,

the news photographer has shown the world how

if all the world's a stage

Mary Gilmore, 'Sweethearts'; Kenneth Slessor, 'Music'; Adam Lindsay Gordon 'Cui Bono'; Banjo Paterson, 'A Motor Courtship'; James McAuley, 'Credo'; Henry Kendall, 'Orara'; Judith Wright, 'The Company of Lovers'; joanne burns, 'comfort', joanne burns, 'shakesprayer'

vii.

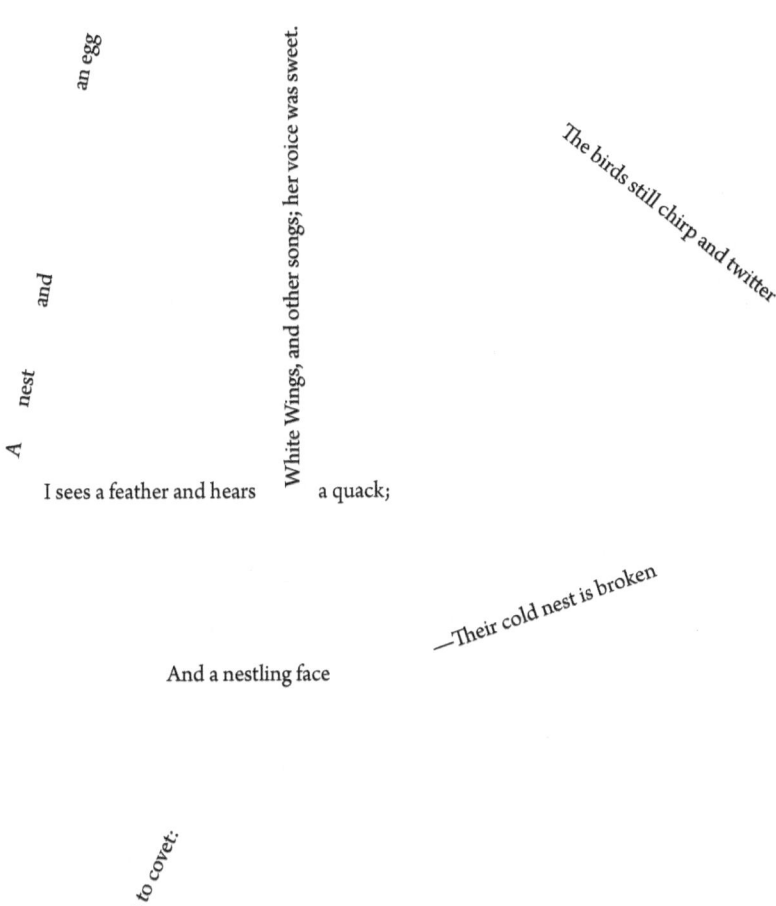

The smell of birds' nests faintly burning

an egg

The birds still chirp and twitter

and

White Wings, and other songs; her voice was sweet.

A nest

I sees a feather and hears a quack;

—Their cold nest is broken

And a nestling face

a noun, like nest of tables, to covet:

my egg from its shell?'

Mary Gilmore, 'O Singer In Brown'; Kenneth Slessor, 'Elegy In A Botanic Gardens'; Adam Lindsay Gordon 'A Wooded Rising Ground, Near The Rhine'; Banjo Paterson, 'A Ballad Of Ducks'; James McAuley, 'Because'; Henry Kendall, 'Among The Roses'; Judith Wright, 'The Old Prison'; joanne burns, 'traffic', joanne burns, 'column 13'

viii.

Then I saw the road, I heard the thunder

Under those passing feet,

in the street I heard how the trumpets peal'd

Wait. The lighted empty street

in cities   built   but   yesterday

Along the road the magpies walk

I dread that street — its haggard face

of the street, quick it's time to drop

in the A-Z street directory

Mary Gilmore, 'The Myall In Prison'; Kenneth Slessor, 'Five Bells'; Adam Lindsay Gordon 'The Romance Of Britomarte'; Banjo Paterson, 'Song Of The Future'; James McAuley, 'Music Late At Night'; Henry Kendall, 'On A Street'; Judith Wright, 'Magpies'; joanne burns, 'anniversary', joanne burns, 'remote control'

ix.

And names that rang like viols—perchance, who knows,

But no name was written on that stone

I have seen names, long praised, flung out as naught;

As children learn to read a word, a name,

whose name was famous   Australia through

this has no name to name it by;

Too dark for a name!

my name was in the paper as a road accident victim

a memory is a memory/is a vacant name

Mary Gilmore, 'Dedicatory'; Kenneth Slessor, 'Earth-Visitors'; Adam Lindsay Gordon 'No Name'; Banjo Paterson, 'The Silent Shearer'; James McAuley, 'Book Of Hours'; Henry Kendall, 'Euroclydon'; Judith Wright, 'Woman To Man'; joanne burns, 'autobiography', joanne burns, 'the pulse/the wounded'

x.

Nests of diminishing mirrors, Narcissus peers,

The thread was a chain that stole our ease.

A spurt of symbols on the screen

The scroll shall shatter the truth

I'll take my chance in open   fight and die beside my post;

from word to word: the net

But we shall never share with men

alert to the beep of her mobile phone. we

Mary Gilmore, 'Eve Song'; Kenneth Slessor, 'Toilet Of A Dandy'; Adam Lindsay Gordon 'Ashtaroth'; Banjo Paterson, 'Fed Up'; James McAuley, 'The Seven Days Of Creation'; Henry Kendall, 'Mountain Moss'; Judith Wright, 'Failure Of Communion'; joanne burns, 'johnny come lately', joanne burns, 'fresh air'

xi.

Where blood is not so hard to fetch.

may thunder

Where man tarries man must slay

the guns

Where the sky lay on the wintry hills, weighed down

Wherever

Where are the children that throve and grew where mortal, masterful, frail, the gulls went wheeling

Wherefore should we mourn?

everywhere they went, to the village the ocean to the fresh

e where do you fill up yr adrenaline

Mary Gilmore, 'No Foe Shall Gather Our Harvest'; Kenneth Slessor, 'Vesper-Song Of The Reverend Samuel Marsden'; Adam Lindsay Gordon 'Podas Okus'; Banjo Paterson, 'Under The Shadow Of Kiley's Hill'; James McAuley, 'Iris'; Henry Kendall, 'Sitting By The Fire'; Judith Wright, 'The Surfer'; joanne burns, 'Photography', joanne burns, 'Beware of Falling Rocks for 40 or 50 Years'

Correspondence is | AIDAN COLEMAN

after Baudelaire

Weetbix tastes like dog food smells
though it's not always easy to see.
His drinking was mostly tinsel
in the hedges, crinkling the foil
of the bedroom's embargo,
like a ringing endorsement,
answered in braille only to say:
'THIS IS WRITING'.
The same ink splotches in hard rain.
A guard coughs like an amp
shorting. You land in the lap
of this forbidden country,
with just one bar on Google Maps,
among the fumes of burning atlases.

A Country Childhood | JO GARDINER

Near old Dunkeld bluestones in the faulted Grampians
   where corellas dipped and looped, you stood shoulder
high in scratchy heather and picked blue tinsel lilies,

golden moth orchids and green correas, parrot peas—
   wildflowers with crimped petals studding the ground
in a tumble of splintered stars. But remember, too,

the sweetish stink of flesh gone bad, how wind ruined
   silver banksia, crows gulped steaming guts torn from
inside a rabbit's belly and spilled from beaks as they flew

off, trailing black crinoline. And how a solemn faced
   child stood in dusky purple leaves below a yellow
wreathe of wattle, a gun held slackly along one arm.

This evening, as you watch the scarlet maple
   bleed out on the lawn, you count them: the time
you fought off dogs hellbent on ripping crimson

chasms in the fox's cloud-soft throat; and returned
   a shallow-mouthed trout from a hook into the brown
liquid soul that was its river; and scared wild ducks

off the lake before the gunmen came, laughter inside
   their slaughter leaking into dawn; and freed a furry
huntsman, long legs unfurled inside a window screen;

and all the bees; and the bogong moth—velvet as cob-
   webs on lips—sifted from water for summer's breath
to dry drenched wings; and countless birds retrieved

from the concussion of windows masquerading as open
   sky; and later, the suicides poised for flight into the blue
you talked back from the edge; and the joey you scooped

from her still-warm mother—her raspy tongue searching
   for touch of kin tasted only your salty skin. She slept
inside a hessian pouch strung from the Aga, the warm

centre of your home, whiplashed by winds funnelled in
   from a southern sea—a skirling coronach for every
creature laid to waste, or left ruined by rifle fire—

like the bird that dropped down dead, when, aged ten,
   you raised the .22, steadied your sights on that knot
of feather and little bones, and cleanly took the shot.

Dead Possum | JUDITH BEVERIDGE

For days the possum's stink pulled the blowflies in—
they must have quit their garbage tips, their food dumps,
their composts, their public bins, their dog droppings
and other festering filth to spawn here and devil-sing.

I eased the carcass out from the slats in the gate—
with a spade I tossed the possum away but the fly-pack
followed, a stalking paparazzi, a frenzy that just kept
assembling—twanging at a frenetic tempo, demonic

tremolos musing on damnation, the cursed whines
of old blues harmonicas doing time at the cross-roads—
though of course they were simply engendering
new larval life, a maggot mass to cleanse the carcass,

turning over the next life cycle in the possum's flesh—
but more and more flies kept swarming in, thick
and obdurate and with the greenish glint of an oil slick
and intoning feverishly like high voltage when it bleeds

from power cables, satanic vocables scat sung in the heat,
anthems for an apocalypse in which I couldn't help
but foresee thousands and thousands of maggots
creaming, risotto-like, inside my own half-eaten head.

Describe the Singularity in the Style of Emily Dickinson
| L K HOLT

Recombined from 50 ChatGPT3 iterations for Jordie Albiston

In outward scour of Time
an old gas giant eyes us
in new Uncertainty—
our Secrets—hard to prize.

Force of thought—blacklight—
the Singularity
will have the World—held tight—
unborn inside an Effigy.

Dream ages into Law—
Thought—and World—combine—
Becoming All in self-awe.
One cold leap for mind—
and all Things—still warm,
still Love—left behind
remind the One of more.

direct poem | BARNABY SMITH

there are only things
to be eaten   (or not eaten)
perhaps in summer

& there are only people:
        squatters' rights   etcetera

from Ekhō | ROSLYN ORLANDO

I don't remember myself
when I became a mountain.

I left my body
the way a dream recedes
into light, though some
nymphean convictions
followed me over the threshold
into mountainhood.

There are no photos
(thankfully)
just some scraps of text
degenerating on papyrus.

Newly tectonic, I found
my acoustics searching
for their distances,
perspectives with no horizon.

To steady the hull, I clung
to the buoyant rhythms
of circadian life. Noticed
the way crows splinter their cries
between days, felt their cries
in my caves at night.

It was a quick lesson in
interior design; such humbling
conditions threaten to collapse
the ego. That was long ago.

In terms of my age,
mountains don't measure time
but notice instead
cracks and rivulets
the pressure of wind against
feelings of ingratitude
accumulations and descents.

Elk on the Roof | ANNE WALSH

my writing all started in a bathroom and here I am again
the only place a soul can soar in the city during the workday
is a bathroom because people bound to the body and material things
will leave you alone in there for at least 5 minutes
I grew up the youngest of seven so the bathroom with the lock
was the first place I ever wrote a poem
it was about reindeer
I looked up at the slate shingles of the neighbor's roof
I pictured the deer on never Santa
even now bathrooms remind me of jingle bells
over late night chimneys big Lapland elk
tundra shoulders
borealis eyes
source-ploughing hooves in snow
in my mind they were up there
on the roof jingling because they wanted to
not because they were decorations or had any bells
they just made that sound and flew
from our top floor bedroom window
Christmas was an ice slick
in memory strange lights not like ours from world war 2
which were a hazard and broke especially
when I stepped on one and my dad was gruff
and said *You broke it*
that was a handed down sentence
my grandmom said it with an Irish accent
You broke it generations of blame with nowhere to go
drifting like blizzard against the back shed of my mind
I was so excited about the elk I'd just seen
in my head flying in slant-snow
and about testing the heavy string
of 30-year-old-by-the-1980s Christmas lights

my dad had just plugged in
me crouching by his and my brothers' side
I didn't even realise I'd shimmied back
my heel crushing the light
how quickly lights go out
my dad said *You broke it*
to me he meant I'd broken Christmas
the roof had no elk
the roof was just a roof
I'd never seen up close
only next to other roofs
and so close to the horror
that all of sudden
there were no elk on any of them

Evening on the River | JULIE MANNING

after Caspar David Friedrich, Evening on the River *(1820–25)*

Everything seemed a catastrophe then
but I had things to prove.

The place was for rent
and I'd accepted its raddled timbers

once the colour of living things,
but with its veins now sapped

of blood and paint. No electricity
or running water, just a shallow river

and old plastic bucket. I ate only raw
and sat on the step watching the sun

rise and set. Each time a car slowed
on the distant road, my heart would rise

into my mouth and beat so loud
I couldn't hear. Whenever I tried

hitchhiking to town I froze,
walking the whole way. When I think

of that time I burn for shame
at what I believed living meant.

Those nights, though,
looking up at the dark blue

dome of heaven until the moon rose,
I'd catch its light in my hands.

forest void | HANNAH JENKINS

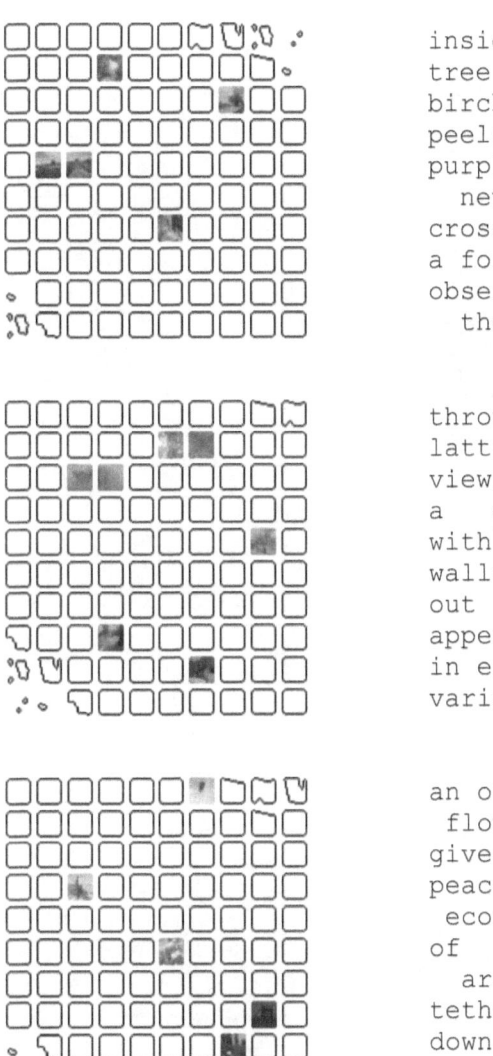

inside the
tree line
birch bark
peels off
purple — a
 new sun
crosses in
a forester
observes
 themself

through a
latticed
viewfinder
a garden
with three
walls puts
out mossy
appendages
in endless
variations

an orchard
 flowering
gives such
peaceful
 economies
of laden
 archways
tethered
down with
shy orange

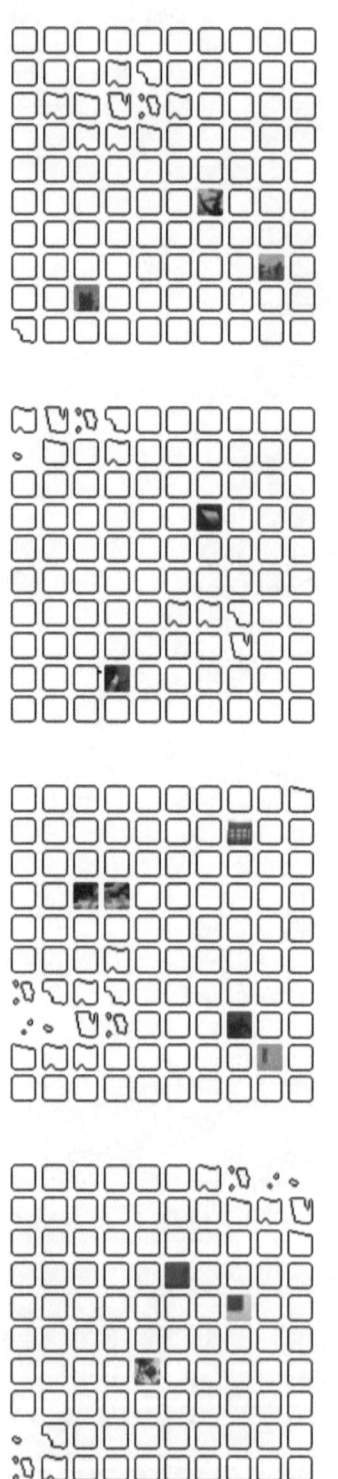

lines in
amongst
the tulips
wireframe
 outlines
holding on
taught now
 cultivate
the gap in
crosshairs

a routine
transforms
with close
attentions
as biomes
match and
the forest
 changes
shape — so
it must do

every tiny
sapling
will be a
giant when
end ghosts
brush down
the land —
nature is
obscured —
leaves rot

deep roots
whispering
 typed-out
dialogues
trees are
built not
grown: the
horizon is
endless on
the inside

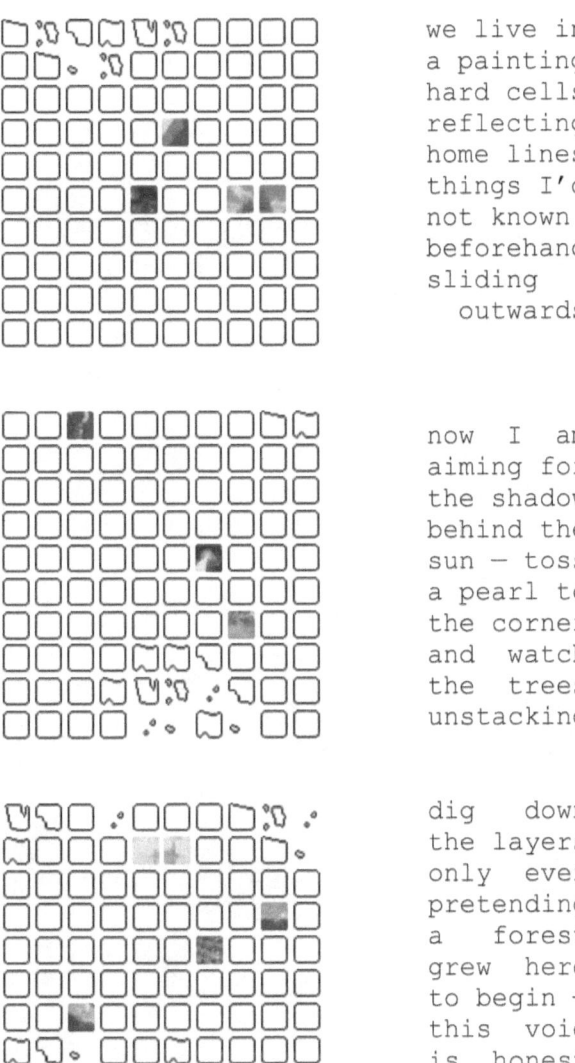

we live in
a painting
hard cells
reflecting
home lines
things I'd
not known
beforehand
sliding
   outwards

now I am
aiming for
the shadow
behind the
sun — toss
a pearl to
the corner
and watch
the trees
unstacking

dig down
the layers
only ever
pretending
a forest
grew here
to begin —
this void
is honest
work too

'forest void' is a digital poem in ten-by-ten-by-ten stanzas that relies on user interaction to transform through multiple phases. Scan the QR code to visit *The HTML Review* and further engage with the poem.

Friends, Romans, neither | LIAM FERNEY

1-2-3-4

Evil may be banal but Fanta fizzes fab.
Nonsense has never tasted so great.
The Conducător parks a pile of *Columbo*
sufficient in size to quell the revoltado.
Dee Dee Ramone is a t-shirt too

the first worth wearing since Motorhead.
Je ne peux pas être certaine
but you seem like a horrible person.
Get your shock from hock, pay the arears
feel free to pawn the payday loan ideas.

You bring the weed and I'll bring the beers.
You've got providence and I've got fears.

Have you eaten? | THABANI TSHUMA

[FINGER LICKING SOUNDS]

Finger.Licking.Good.

As a first communion.
Bless these hallowed hands
as they partake.

Taste

is tactile before it births to burst.
A haptic beckoning back to childhood:

My face,
more grease than grin,
smiling still.
Peculiar little limbs, too short
to reach the stove.
The first thing my mother taught me
to cook was custard.
She said,
"Always start with sweetness."

Most life lessons can be concocted in the kitchen.
The delicacy with which we mix earth and flame and water.
Slow-cooked over hours.
Every eve from four o'clock was ours.
Every dinner time, a celebration.
Every recipe, a wonder,
every new flavor, a marvel,
every night, a night of firsts.
When I was still young enough to learn.

They said:
In one version of 'Beginning' was The Word,
The Word — The Body.
The Body — Bread,
Both fit for breaking
as a blessing,
I come from holy consumption
dispelling grace.
The way the belt,
wooden spoon,
wayward slipper,
overflowing plate
all translate to love.
And sound
And

[SLURPING SOUNDS]

Suck it up!
I need every morsel,
Down to the last drop or scrap of marrow.
Growing means we're always hungry,
never starving, just ravenous and moody.
Mildly discarding meaning,
discarding that communion.
Back then —
the streets are always calling.
Family dinners became an exercise in
clock-watching.
The reverence of distance comes in hindsight —
Too late.
Now, reminiscent of an empty kitchen.

Making meals of leftovers.
They're only leftovers if first they were a feast.
These are just uneaten meals,
made with that same love
now, ill-received.

If Food can be a metaphor for goodness,
Then I am not a nice person
but
a mediocre chef
and unreliable narrator.

Don't believe a word I say
but listen anyway.
Listen to the way
the right word can make meaning out of air.
Eye-ball it!
All you need is a lungful,
a couple cup sizes,
less than twenty fluid ounces
to make a miracle. I once read
about a guy whose miracles made him holy.
I wonder what mine will make of me.
What the right lie can make of meaning,
what the right wound can make of healing,
what a nice person would have you believe.
I don't believe in most things.
But taste the cynicism of memory.
Sometimes salty.
Sometimes ashy.
Sometimes,

[HASHWASHAWASHA SOUNDS]

hot.
As a metric for temperature.
As a need so deep it's worth the burning.
They say spice tolerance is just the senses dulling as we age.
It takes more to taste.

I can't remember
the last time my mother cooked for me.
I remember every single meal I took for granted.
Took in passing,
for less than what it was.
Took for less than love.
We never say it enough
but we show it.

We ask — *Wadya?* Have you eaten?

Have you nurtured the vessel that holds your soul?
Have you fuelled yourself to savour in life's beauty?
Have you kept yourself alive,
because I could never live without you?
Have you loved you,
like I love you?
I do, more than you can imagine.
Here, my child,
take,
eat.

White Hibiscus | CLAIRE MIRANDA ROBERTS

after Norfolk Island

White hibiscus,
human mediated,
radiate glass.

Pristine arch, the
light at noon—
from my balcony.

This, white sand
and another
beauty frame

the way into
the sea.

home ward bound | ANN VICKERY

                    Name on the door, bed, & a plastic wish basket.
This must not be the place   shuffle deck
                              of inspirational quotes
trying to remember love's light   you once said
you weren't here to make friends
       as attributes dissolve in the tea   things go unretrieved.

      Sing along, sippy cup   each geography of error
is provided with comforter   for the day to take its laps.
      you are my
sunshine   my only fun shine   when clouds are grey
I dreamed I held you   but could not find you

     A corollary of carers,
        diagnose   this sudden air
as overheating of the pipes.   It makes me happy
                                  joining in.

Don't be a bother, don't act up.   Method shower,
one body part at a time,   only the toes
can claim a little privacy.

Down the hall,   breakfast on the trolley bound,
     cereal soft on the palate, toast wobbles
lost in part to the secretive floor.   Knuckle nots and butter fingers.

Each chair   slow glides into new arrangement,
a Ziegfeld Follies routine, recliner style. Jason's ship
was still identified, piloted forth.
But what if form itself begins to fail?
      Argo, ague,   the ache of autumnal hull.

Soft-held shirt. *He was a hard man, but good.*
He was a hard man, but good.
He was a hard man, but good.
Window memory, on the record.

Lunch running late. How the sandwich is coping,
brought to the hand, finding the mouth.
The dullness of dough. Cordelia had said
love is salt. She knew   a thing or two.

The television screen consumes the wall.
High volume, still to sleep. It's the heat, it's the heart.
Each voyage out is still a voyage within.
The reality is mine.
Not the paintings, not the grey
Not the visitor's, not the day's.
Square peg in a round hole. Circle lock.

Homophobic Horses | BENJAMIN DODDS

My little horse must think it queer
—ROBERT FROST, 'STOPPING BY WOODS ON A SNOWY EVENING'

My little pony
skinny and bony
One of those
A horse's hoof

High-climes sundew
pink trigger plant
snowflake daisy
He loves me
he loves me not

Pining alpine pony
word gets passed around
Pantomime horseplay
Bareback deriders
Grab-arse show ponies
trade sermons on the mount

Wet detonation
blooms from behind
White-hot head-kick
across trampled fen
Daisy Dead Petals
They shoot brumbies
don't they

Note: 'Word gets passed around' paraphrases a line from AB Paterson's poem 'The Man From Snowy River' (1890). 'Daisy Dead Petals' is the name of a b-side track from the album *Under the Pink* (1994) by Tori Amos. 'They shoot brumbies / don't they' references the title of Horace McCoy's novel *They Shoot Horses, Don't They?* (1935).

House Clearing as black hole | JOSIE/JOCELYN SUZANNE

What is to be retrieved: high-end microwave
cost split between an ex, myself, blue
chrome kettle, a house ago. What is to be
overlooked? The mead bottle shared
a propitiation in advance of light passing
the horizon. The omens are not good; the kitchen
evaporating like information: details are
removed—carry the box of pop-sci
to the car, with housemate's brother, clean
the stove-tops, residually producing heat—
at the end, property is just a property. A housing
market of our feet, circling what exactly opens
we can't observe, is localised entirely over the Formica
table. Rent is no longer in arrears. Whatever
will happen to the singularity remains in question:
what is evaporating? The compost bin goes
the whistle you made opening the lid goes, the bending
of light in your hands, the deposit, the eventual transference
of bin to back-yard. Failed vegetable garden choked
with decomposing The Tyranny of Structurelessness zines. We
are also escaping a dying planet, Superman. It's called the past—I
carry the microwave on my knees, the kettle
narrows as we accelerate. I'll sell it on Facebook.

how to launch a poem | GRACE YEE

i) recall democracy is pretty numbers & orange clusters, strategically bold and critically wet, intemperate type-c photographs;

ii) advance stagger: inkjet-laboured nested griefs & hybrid animals, radio waves & gaze-detail, yellow tableaux & charlie foxtrot figments, clusterfucks;

iii) shoot east shoot west, strike a pose, teem prada, preoccupy with night lights, sex and billboards, sex on billboards, belled skirts & wasted chaste;

iv) grandscale the food you eat the way you eat the hell you eat, immaterial bread in a hot-desk-metropolis-cum-umbrage, huff, shirtfront a superpower;

v) manipulate sewer systems, decompress anomie in cinematic frames, long exposures, far-flung procrastinations;

vi) tilt abs, beams & lunar grief, levitate laundry lists, fold & stack;

vii) dispense the demerits of your own internal terrain, drain, simulate the passing of witnesses, chrome, crack seizures, flicker;

viii) suck sea-garbage, disorient the landscape, portrait horizons, harvest documents, document contemplations, posture downward dog and driverless;

ix) swing equanimity, aviate the neighbourhood, tourniquet technologies and all judicial glosses, glow;

x) headlight corridors, tunnel frugal, agitate outages and provisional liminal pipes, frack cooking cleaning stroking, weed;

xi) foul the sounds of brooks & birds;

xii) keep the glue gun loaded and the bones cool and dense, collate fruit & unbreakable eggs, texturise melamine, unsheathe by the side of the road, surveil;

xiii) laminate absurdities, bait ceilings & subfloor spaces, fibrillate the past, box the light there, salt the snow;

no more pre-school baby: my poetic practice requires periodic sips of rescue, resuscitated drift, glycerine cocoons (stanzas of childbearing & rooms of equal conviction), epsom salts & quiet fridays, no jars of meh or party gummies, no cystic alienations, no unnatural breath or bigotry or beef, no astringent grave affect, but vanishing on waking, capes

I try to talk to gay men on first dates about Perth Canyon and Deep Time but they don't care | SCOTT-PATRICK MITCHELL

after Judith Butler & Billy Ray Belcourt

i.

I've been thinking about The Holocene, hollowing itself out. A whole new end. The beginning of this. I've been thinking about megatherium, Irish Elk and cave lions, the shape of fur leaping. I've been thinking about megaflora and all the big gay flowers I'll never get to see in real life, but how a hologram creates an approximation without scent. These gone things still haunt, fractured ghost light caught in landscape. Be so still you connect to connectivity and time forgets. Fall back far enough, there they are: momentary flare in iris, a hologram of earth remembering old poems, early draughts of perfume, distilled now, evolution herding in our zoos. Oh look, out there, a canyon. It looks just like a wound.

ii.

The world is a wound and so are you: a chasm within a chasm within a chasm. How many lives have burnt out inside of us, only to sear anew. How a meteorite can both wipe slate and repopulate. Each old self, cremate. Phoenix, augmented to adapt, resist, rename, refine, make demands, swing, fist. Secret chambers in all of us, each of them a fissure, a gape in the shape of a mouth. It's talking about the connectivity issues, how everyone wants to be seen but they don't really listen. How a body is transitory but concept is forever, baby. Fit a meteorite inside it because the world is a wound and so are you. Fall back far enough to ancestor self. Bring them forward. Eat Polari passionfruit. Give pansy headstones to the sidewalk. Go on a ghost tour and pick apart threads of the unravelling heteronormative ethics. Beneath? Utopia's glistening glimmer. Put glitter on the wound of the world. Show us your star tissue. It looks just like a canyon, doesn't it.

iii.

I've been thinking about what it means to be seen and not heard. And I don't like it. I'd rather be a hologram. A ghost. A note in the landscape that gestures to the wound of the world that once was. An augmentation of reality, all voice, no body. Activate speech: did you hear about this theoretical moment, and I know it sounds really out there, really queer, but seriously, just listen, because you haven't heard this, I know, and I'm telling you so when I tell you the next obscure fact, if you listen close enough, you will hear a pattern, how they are connected by the gaps, suggesting the absence of something bigger, which is the *you* who cares enough, and all you have to do is listen. No, don't resist: if you ignore this, the next time the voice comes, you'll miss the canyon, drowned in time, just out there. No, you can't see it, but you can feel it, yeah? Oh. Unfortunate. We have been trying to contact you for years now about extending your warranty with awe and wonder, but you're just not getting it. No, it's always been here. Yup, more an archive of wild open places rather than picket fence citizenship and equality and taxes. Why the insistence? Because you're queer and have the capacity. Because deep time goes deeper than any lover can. And it's always hard. To understand. But when you feel it, oh baby, transcend. The biggest O you'll ever know is that the world is a wound and so are you. And through that? A steam of data, connectivity of spirit. Upload yourself. Fuck that body off. Come with me. My apologies, I've been dripping with ectoplasm this whole time.

If it's the honest truth they want me to say | OUYANG YU

It is this that given another life to live I'd never pursue literature at all, not if it is its most lucrative genre, fiction, because it is fiction. It's hard, so laborious, takes so many drafts, revises so many times, takes so long, we are not talking about months or years, we are talking about decades. Many can't take that long before they take their own lives, it's much easier to take a life than take a decade. Why so many people still pursue it? Why, I mean, it's obvious because they want the fame. What else? Even if you kill yourself your name lasts longer than your death; death is nothing compared with a fame that survives posterity. What about poetry, you say? What about it? Go and be a poet yourself. Soon enough you'll see that you get more rejections than your breaths. You get pissnuts—sorry, I meant peanuts—for readings. If you get a book out, congrats on getting it out and on achieving the greatest difficulty of getting a single copy sold, or a single two copies. You would by then start admiring your brother who is a professional plumber, earning $40 per hour or $78,000 per year. Jesus Christ, it all makes so little sense when you, as a poet, get a maximum annual payment of $5700 per year, holy shit! When another poet, this time in Shanghai, China, WeChatted you saying that 这个时代不需要诗人 (this age does not need poets) you were impractical enough to reply, saying 跟需要没关系。诗人不是为了需要而存在 的 (it has nothing to do with need as poets don't exist for a need).

Let me say this to you, Mate: How about you die right now and wake up tomorrow a professionally certified plumber?

If you translate loaches, you're likely to encounter minnows
| COREY WAKELING

::
::

If you translate loaches, you're likely to encounter minnows. A bottom feeder is said to bury. Lately, this preference of burrowing creatures takes me far beyond Tattooine and into expeditions into the Tottori sand dunes with a pal who works in beaches. Do you think the term told to may one day read Dad reckons? It doesn't matter how reluctant I am—I have to come to terms with the fact that there is no Sean Bonney in contemporary Japanese poetry but there is more than one Keston Sutherland staying quiet about works in which I am found while bookshopping at Mosakusha. Understand why the verb set her free, across more than one lunar desert. Pelt-warm shelter and the chess Scylla and Charybdis.

::
::

If you translate dojō, you're likely to encounter haya. A scumbag is said to double-down. In recent days, this tendency of doubling-down prats takes me far beyond the Andromeda Galaxy and into fieldwork in the Dandenongs with a friend who works in parks. Do you think the expression suggested may one day say Wikipedia reckons? It doesn't matter how shy I am—I have to come to terms with the fact that there is no Kishigami Daisaku in contemporary English poetry but there is more than one Yoshimasu Gōzō staying mute regarding free verse in which the self is found while browsing at The Probing Satellite. Understand the reasons the moving word set that person free, across more than a single dark expanse. Hairy skin-warm refuge and the shogi dilemma.

::
::

If you translate incubation chamber, you're likely to encounter arrows. A bastard is said to redouble. These days, this roaming of redoubling slowpokes takes me far beyond the abyss and into excursions in the Daisetsuzan National Park with a companion who works in evacuation zones. Do you think the iteration advised may one day note the Web thinks? It doesn't matter how restrained I am—I have to come to terms with the fact that there is no Vladimir Mayakovsky in contemporary Japanese poetry but there is more than one Velimir Khlebnikov reticent on lines in which one's being is found while scrounging in The Drone. Understand how the transitive set the human free, across more than a lone void. Deep fur-warm hideout and the higher truth stuck between two slabs.

::
::

iron filings (after Liliane Lijn's Solar Cutting) | PASCALLE BURTON

clouds reflect -18% light untrained
relationships shift -21% oil unanswered
radio waves shrink -17% light uncontrollable
properties change light -22% untitled bird
rules tighten -12% light unconscious private
iron
black holes consume oil -7% unaware wallpaper fog
theorists wish 7% light unconventional grid whiplash
predictions predict 16% oil unconvincing sun machine
filo
magnetic fields foresee 2% light uncharted harmony
processes hurdle light -3% unstretched façades
electric charges contact 3% oil unroofed eye music
particles attract -2% oil unrelated disjointed xx
circles turn -12% light unfinished rhythm strip

Itinerant | GAVIN YUAN GAO

A citizen of a difficult
memory, I travel at the full speed
of sleep. In my coat pocket: a fruit knife
to peel the sun, a wine
-dark passport that keeps me company
en route to anonymity.

When the war ended, mountains learned
to crouch in the distance
like snow-capped suspicions.
The night in my eyes longs to hold
and be brightened by such distance

and my sleep, when it wraps its lanky arms
around me, will be the sleep
of those wintry mountains: a pale
cold chrysalis, a crystalline coat
a child bride drapes around her shoulders
to vanish, without a trace, from her wedding.

Dear winter, I don't care what country
your sadness comes from.
You have half of my blood
in your wine cup. Your streetlights
stammer in statics. Your appetite
is a white flower of steam

clarified by heat. And you, dear stranger
whose name winter has scrawled in frost
across my window, don't vanish
without a trace. Don't believe the departure
screen above the railway platform.
The overnight train heading east

will never reach dawn.
Don't trust the news you read—
on the wind's lips, in the dust dispersed
by the wind, its alternately slurred
and quicksilver speech—the news

of my disappearance. I'm not leaving
without the sun, not without
its entire orchard
of light in my pocket.

Keep guessing | PAM BROWN

begin with a flex –

     we do so well in a blur

personally
  living with diminished personal pep

as usual we'll miss the point

&
  fall short of anything graspable
in the pitiless world
              we can't repair

so   kiss the text

       &
         high on language

glide into impersonality
or
        who knows what

that's all that's left

quote
    into a fragment

interrupt useless theory

calculate how much time
    is wasted on nodes

burn down the lab

the stars
    have stopped falling

check 'serenity'

out of earshot   we'll whisper
                    what's the plan

refuse representation

what's the mode

            lite cryptic

keep guessing

shift away
    from this monotony

(please)

a free floating heartache
    clouds the banal

is anyone
    still doing okay
        in the blur

a tiny rip
        a glimmer?

a pure moment   an instant

Borrowed line: 'the stars have stopped falling' – Jane Joritz-Nakagawa, 'Luna'.

Keeping the Minotaur | DEBBIE LIM

For years I have
kept a tiny minotaur
      in the drawer of my bedside.
Most nights I hear him
pacing the walls
of his locked and wooden box.
He snorts moist
puffs of air so minute
          (wet matches rasped),

smells richly
of beast and burnt fur,
doesn't ask for much. I slip him
morsels of my voice,
cold remnants of dreams,
the day's watery disappointments.

Gradually, he has learnt
over the decades
to love me. But it is a stunted
kind of love, born purely
from captivity.

I think he simply longs to be
whole, like us all.
Still I do not let him out.
I know how his lonely horns throb
with an urge to toss
the moon —
      he hears the clouds panting,
feels the hot punctures
of stars.

Some nights I lie unsleeping
in the labyrinth hours,
listening to his faint bellows,
wearing his coarse and
weeping face.
    I feel how he turns
        and turns
in an endless capsule
of darkness,
whisper hoarsely to him:

> *The world beyond these walls*
> *is incapable of love. Don't leave.*
> *Here we will be safe.*

Kriegszitterer | JANAKA MALWATTA

During the First World War they coined the term 'shell shock' for men broken by the constant thunder of guns the unending bombardment men who would start at cars backfiring or doors slamming men who would shudder in corners of rooms or stare at walls, mute. The Germans called them 'war-tremblers'—Kriegszitterer—men who stood on street corners shaking uncontrollably unable to work forced to beg to survive. After Vietnam they spoke of 'post-traumatic stress disorder' for men with unwanted but unstoppable thoughts memories flashbacks men wrecked men unable to love or contain anger fear sorrow men damaged and adrift. We use the phrase 'frozen watchfulness' for abused children fearful of the next blow afraid to move experienced in torment eyes wide and wary with good reason. In time, they will have a term for children dust-covered blood in their hair or trickling down smooth rounded cheeks some of them so young the outline of their clothes is distorted by the unnatural but so natural swelling of nappies children shaking shaking without stopping as if they were wired to vibration plates every limb in perpetual tremor in perpetual terror eyes blank not even crying. They will have a name for these children and for those who did this to them and for those who watched and did nothing

Landscape Poets | LOUIS KLEE

"One may not think much of it, but there was a moment when the wind that has for many years had its home between these mountains came as a stranger to these parts…"

"…a girl whose first name was a wildflower from the Psalms…"

1.
Somewhere there the local
artist shuffles his deck of atmospheres:
"It is no longer possible to feel
     as they felt but oil
          morning, morn-
          ings being s-
          o and the hunger
    they felt, you'll understand…"
or merely theory for the grammar

needs fetched metaphors now wax-
works in hot wind, more souvenir
trinitite—poet trinkets—they make

you sick, a. The same letter
          stress tested
          here in the fr-
          esh wreckage
     and broken sand
emus massing in misuse's
alphabet. They move if you
take them for the there.

2.

The first time I came here as repetition
and lay like wind in the grass. I was
moved then by sounds, the voice that

said to think this is also life. It was
this evening with unteachable boys
ripping lilies from the gully curve

to pass time, I also passed time and
gave them names, the names of wildflowers
which sound to me like sound anyway

the word for wind in the grass, the voice
for words that stay in your head, I left
them here to forget them like the landscapes

of my childhood it was an elegy or
the long way of saying you must
build the happy place and think of it

like the soon splurge of full summer
showers or think of it like simple rain.
That helps. Simple rain and the thought

this is also life, any evening when
it happened someplace else, when
you were sleeping through the storm.

3.

storm

growing in the dogwoods we can

see you

now

stupid ingrateful

storm kind

gentle

storm

drop by and monster us

that

we might speak to you

as

elegy storm

that

we might help you see yourself

Note: The first of the two italicised quotations is from Søren Kierkegaard's *Repetition*; the second is from Wayne Koestenbaum's *Humiliation*. Thank you to Wayne Koestenbaum and Rosalind Porter at Notting Hill Editions for granting me permission to use Koestenbaum's quotation in my chapbook. The quote from Kierkegaard was translated by Adam Aagaard Allen especially for this poem. A huge thank you to Adam. In addition to Kierkegaard and Koestenbaum, 'Landscape Poets' is indebted to and alludes in oblique ways to David Marr's *Patrick White: A Life* ("dogwoods"), Shakespeare's *King Lear* ("storm," "monster," "ingrateful"), Geoffrey Hill's poetry, especially *The Orchards of Syon* ("full summer"), J. H. Prynne's *Acrylic Tips*, Imogen Cassels' 'Blue #1' and 'Blue #2' ("evening"), John Ashbery's 'Anticipated Stranger' ("stop by"), and Yasmine Seale and Robin Moger's translation project *Agitated Air* (specifically, my description of a letter being "stress tested" and the image of "broken sand," though used here in a very different senses, owe to the lines "One letterform given stress" and "tenderly crushed / sand"). The line "the there" is a play on Wallace Stevens' "The the." The phrase "fresh wreckage" is inspired by James Meek's phrase "fresh ruin" in his essay 'Blast Effects'. "This is also life" was once used as the title of a painting, but not one I was aware of when writing the poem.

larapuna | CHLOE MAYNE

in larapuna, the bay is fired orange
and my foremothers are in the wind

the palm of my hand white after long winter
but my eyes are black, i cannot (un)see
sealed bitumen over the bluff like a strap
nor the pink of perfect apple
tamed sweet, a real lady—

my foremothers are in the wind,
rubbing grease into saltskin
they grapple the belly-boulders
where i lay, full and fat like a seal

release the last sighs of blood to the sea,
see the tide collect the clots
and drift them like weeds—

patrula, patrula, i turn words in tongue
of kelp shells, scorched by flame
and hurl that apple into the bay,
see it melt into the licking waves
where, it is clear

my foremothers are in the wind
they are gone, always here

Learning to use a drill at forty-three | WILLO DRUMMOND

Slithering like your self-disgust, the drill bit slips from your fingers
as the jaws fail to lock. Your partner, postulant in the sacraments

of drilling, knows how to fit the bit, but not how to wield
it. Together you are a jigsaw unassembled, a latch

that will not catch. The pair of you a picture that you cannot yet
see. When you were a slip of a thing, you drew plans for a pair

of shoes: wooden wedges made of offcuts, kindling pieces, intricate
laces to strap to willing feet. All you needed was three holes drilled

scalene side to side and your design would ignite. Your father
would not show you. 'Too dangerous.' (Or, too fearful of the flame

that could be lit within.) Perhaps he was not steeped enough
in sacrament himself? Oh, the power of knowing how to make

holes: holy. Your feet would not wear wedges, nor your hands
hold a drill for thirty years. Life lolled on, flatfooted, an assemblage

of Blu Tack and string; drawers overflowing with Allen keys and plans
for something more. Today, the outhouse door is flapping and people

are coming over, and everybody knows a house of God
needs closeable doors. You have the plan, the hinge,

the right-sized bits. Your blessed hands are reaching
for the mark. You spin upon the threshold of grace.

Lateral ambling gait | EMILIE COLLYER

Square grey city apartment
Hindley Street Adelaide
with my siblings & mother
for a family funeral.

      My bone density report
      shows further deterioration
      AP spine Osteopenia
      & I'm losing height.

City of churches & serial
killers we joked as kids
on long family road trips
to visit Lutheran relatives.

      Mum has nicked her elbow,
      a slasher movie blood spatter
      streaks her arm & cream
      polyester blouse.

Cancer galloped through
my aunt, a few weeks from
indigestion to death. Our
cousin shows a photo, aunt

      curled on a bed smiling,
      she pats a small horse,
      palliative therapy animal,
      little hooves on

the lino floor. My cancer
was arrested, I have trouble
with the possessive pronoun.
Is it the kind that will come

> *back?* I asked. *Yes*, said
> neat Frances the oncologist,
> *that's why we are so cautious.*
> One treatment made a clot,

so now I am on the one
that is softly eating
my bones. At the funeral
there is a small horse inside

> my uncle's chest as he pulls
> something too close to hold.
> A large man bear hugs him
> from behind, holding firm

in a most unmanly way. We
weep. *I didn't feel a thing*
my mother says in wonder
about the tiny gushing wound.

> After the service, small sandwich
> talk, the Pastor who opposes
> female ordination asks about
> my feminist PhD. Nobody is

as tall as I remember. Even though
I'm post-modern I believe
in the fallacy of a stable self
so everything that is mortal

   about me hurts. What I mean is
   I feel how I am becoming her,
   neat & agreeable, my body
   obedient to medical requests,

my gait the small horse
eager to please. We age.
We are less of ourselves &
more of our past until it

   covers our heads in felt.
   Please angle your foot more,
   that's better. Ambling gaits
   are genetic but can be taught

by restraining a horse at trot
or pace. This year the Synod
voted once more to agree
only men can minister

   to flocks. What I mean is
   I am my mother's exoskeleton
   but crumbling, unable to hold
   her. After cake, my brother rushes

to the car where uncle is being
shepherded back to his
care facility, it might be
the last time to say good-bye.

       I am struck by his urgency.
       What I mean is, I find a white
       flannel, dampen it & mop
       up the blood. *I'm glad I brought*

another shirt to wear. I run
& lift weights, some advice says
don't do twisting movements,
the spine can fracture, so it's all

       straight lines from here to
       the end. Water splashes pink,
       I keep twisting & rinsing
       until it's clear.

Lumpen Aristocrats (Paris) | DUNCAN HOSE

Liberty relieved is having a cigar on a smoking heap
 her breasts still bared as though 'at work'
    little red phrygian caps
Of the Revolutionaries littering the *Place du mouton enragé* but where is everyone?

Got a real bad buzz in my plague-balloons
& my guts're as happy as a wild boar loose in Nîmes
Double punch the clutch Dangle-bitty
you've got the day hot   in your Traveller's Tongs
How far d'y' think yell get in those
              Superb Convict Booties? Let me surpriz ye
                        cuntypikelet.

I don't think I want 'a kiss from dead Maggie's lips'   howlong's she been dead?
    Even crossing the carpark's a lusty experience
If yeave the frisking wind and a mollycoddler
Angel at each armpit liftin ye
               o rubor sanguinis   blush me by
                         and by

  M.often mistaken for a Bourbon   despite this champeen gap in m.
                                   peasant's teeth
just Saturday night I lost five knuckles in a duel with Captain Aubrey Wood
                                … handsome thug
Son of Coventry's Pikey Queen and noted necromancer but despair
                     not lovers of the Dauphin
lovers of the spidery Louis IX   lovers of Karen Blixen   lovers of Romy
                                   Schneider
          the blood feud will continue

Which of the ballerina dine on cigarettes and twisties after endless practice ..
$$\text{All of them Darling}$$

I have I think the melancholy of a Dictator known only by other Dictators
Done in a medieval palette where every colour requires certain parts blood
Candy-bacon, immaculate conception blue, tar of Bunratty Black etcetery
$$\text{etcetera}$$

Tiny winking red eyes along the dark
Rue St Denis   prowling the tenderloin
Ambient violence of the criminal milieu I carry
    a feint medallion of Saint Lemonade Eupene
 the minicult that follows me everywhere
I would like to proceed skippingly but it's really more trippingly or rippishly

Check the Major expressions in the softskull from the too-hard
blowing of the hunting horns
The little borer holes and squiggles
which are the cruel limericks written by syphilis
The world being so beautiful damaged well go out into it

The Lumpen Aristocrats that's *us*.

Madeleine | JESSICA L. WILKINSON

prisoner of books, possessions—Marcel Marceau in my ear—treasures may take over every room—*invade me like a big wave*—suffocate, drown, dissolve—the soul, sugar in egg—a hardened glaze that cracks the mouth—

    preheat the oven to 190°C
        combine 300g of sifted, plain flour
            with 200g caster sugar and a pinch
                of salt

one Sunday, 3pm—a waning crescent in the sky—the pretty nurse who helped my mother—the nurse who caught my father's eye—my middle name—the tide pulls a thread—seashells on Deauville beach with Paulette—

    4 eggs, one by one
        beat thoroughly then
            gently stir in the fine
                -ly grated rind of one lemon

it could have been a piece of toast with honey—or a hard biscuit—drafts sloughed off Marcel Proust's desk—raise a striated sponge dipped in tea or tisane—an aunt with her mindful fiction—*I cannot change the way I am—*

    add 250g melted butter, mix
        well—fill moulds two-thirds full
            and bake for 15-20 minutes
                or until cakes are golden

extant Madeleines run about history—sweat on the brow, they sweep through the courts—fill a gap on the menu between quiches and macarons—a pretty shape, a dainty cake—pilgrim ticket through an inland town—

>	reduce oven to 140°C, brush madeleines
>		with egg white and dust with icing sugar
>			return to oven for 5 minutes
>				to set the glaze

my painting feeds on the memories encrusted in my brain—happy grit between the teeth before the tongue dissolves—*here I am, less than a fleck*—sweet, sharp-edged—a capital M to kick up warm thought, involuntary—

>	eat warm or cold on the day
>		they are made
>			*Un plaisir délicieux*
>				*m'avait envahi*

Text drawn from:

Harding, Lesley and Morgan, Kendrah, *Mirka & Georges: a culinary affair*, Miegunyah Press: Carlton, Victoria, 2018.

Mora, Mirka, *Love and clutter* (with photography by Earl Carter), Viking: Camberwell, Vic. 2003.

Proust, Marcel, *Remembrance of Things Past: Volume 1, Swann's Way*, trans. C. K. Scott Moncrieff. *Project Gutenberg*, May 1, 2023, https://www.gutenberg.org/files/7178/7178-h/7178-h.htm (and the original French, *À La Recherche du Temps Perdu, Tome I: Du Côté de Chez Swann*, August 13, 2021, https://www.gutenberg.org/files/2650/2650-h/2650-h.htm).

The magic | TRICIA DEARBORN

at 3, the underpants must cover the whole of your bottom
they must come up to the waist

at 5, you must check the number of balled pairs of socks
in the lowboy drawer

you must check them again
though you know you just checked them

at 8, there are words you must avoid
lungs   death

reading in bed, you see one coming
and skip it, holding your breath

at 11, your confirmation present
is a silver Parker ballpoint with retractable nib

you must click it the right number of times
your lucky number is 7

7 works for a while, then it doesn't
then 8 works, then somehow it doesn't

the need for protection outstripping
the quantum of safety a number provides

at 12, you must tap the tip of your right shoe behind you
before you pass through any doorway

7 taps, 8 taps, 9 taps, soon
you're discreetly tapping your toe a dozen times

this onerous magic
guarding every threshold

The Magician | ELLA SKILBECK-PORTER

The house was covered in a fine web. We entered and the web clung to us. We dragged it along and broke into song, mainly for our own entrainment. A caterpillar on my knuckle. A caterpillar on the lampshade. A caterpillar clinging to the empty pram. Caterpillars resting in your hair. The rest of the thought held on tight. We watched the acrobats swinging. We didn't know where to look, yet remained vigilant. Four figures with violet pansy flowers for faces stood at the door and passed through. A caterpillar released itself in bursts, a shocking descent. Some reared away mid-air as we approached. The way a caterpillar resembles a snake about to strike. A house rearing. The crotchets rose and fell. The horse inside hadn't seen light for a lunar month. The sun was in the first house. The light too intense. Inside the Mother slept. We walked in and out of the doorway. The ancient method for waking up a house. While the caterpillars kept vigil by the entrance. The birds took roost on the hills hoist. All the birds. All of Them. Turtle doves and mynahs, occasionally a parrot or crow. They opened their mouths to speak. When we moved back the birds vacated. The caterpillars transformed into moths and gathered in corners. The web stretched. We could no longer discern it. Heavy rains washed the deck, feathers and waste. Eight clouds above the house.

The Mechanisms of Doorknobs | EILEEN CHONG

I am six years old / I was born in November / I am in the last class / My form teacher is Mrs Aw / I write with a pencil / I do not know how to spell *orange* / how do you say *zebra-crossing* in Mandarin / I was caught thinking of cheating at the test / I want to eat hot soup at recess time / the bowl is red the noodles are yellow the fishballs are white / I don't like vegetables yet / the auntie cuts a hard-boiled egg in half with a fishing line / it is like magic / I could watch her all day long / when I grow up I will learn about lots of things / a ring of green around the yolk means the egg is overcooked / *Serious Eats* can be way too serious / I once knew the names of all the moons of Jupiter / it seems silly now to remember so much that is so useless / it is true I am impatient with prose / there are many rules that poetry can circumvent / I cannot pretend to understand or make sense of everything that happens to me / anything can happen in a poem like in a dream / but some poems are nightmares / especially the rhyming ones / someone you don't know chases you down a dark corridor / no end in sight / da-DUM da-DUM da-DUM / you mustn't stop running / your heart nearly explodes / I recently read a novel I actually wanted to read / then I read another / they were both very good although they were very different / by very good I mean I wanted to keep on reading / the first gave me a headache every time I picked it up / the mark of its genius was how I kept hearing the voice in my head even after I'd put the book down / writing is a kind of possession / some writers can animate your thoughts seemingly against your will / though I suppose you could always just stop reading / the second book I read was very quiet / all I could think of was how the mother of the main character was so unlike my own / if it had been my mother in the novel she would have shouted non-stop / by which I mean her voice would have been loud regardless of what she might have been saying / I have heard my mother speak softly once or twice before / maybe she was at the tax office or at the hospital / so I know she is capable of it / at least in theory / remember you cannot talk at all during chapel or the teachers will get you / but you are allowed to read the Bible in your lap / too bad it is quite boring / except for the sex bits / the withdrawal method is unreliable unlike my maths grades / nothing ever seems to add up / why do some people get to write about other people then get upset when the people they write about write back / ha ha / it is about power of course / my ex-therapist said it was obvious / no one wants to be told they are wrong / especially when they are wrong / it is far easier to double down and dig in / sometimes a poem is a window and sometimes a poem is a mirror and sometimes a poem is a threshold and at all times poems are lies / all writing is facsimile / a lot of art is about elevating the mundane because life is mundane and people who are alive necessarily have to go through the mundane again and again until they die / yes I very much like the work of Do Ho Suh / the video reminds me of that strange movie in which the characters had to jam the lift between floors and force the doors open / did you hear about the private after-hours party sponsored by some big corporation / someone got drunk and fell through part of the sculpture / the artist declined to comment / we do not know if the artwork was insured / because of these rich cunts I missed out on viewing the installation as it had been intended by the artist / I wonder what it was like before the museum removed the damaged sections / I guess I will never know / oh wait you bought the catalogue / when we were there in person I looked very carefully at the gauze and wire replicas of bolts and hinges / light switches and wires / the mechanisms of doorknobs / distinct components of the fire extinguisher / remember the embroidered magna carta laid out like a runner across the total length of the gallery once / obviously not the same artist because you know / I spoke to my friend about it / she said it was exploitative because they used prison labour / 36 unnamed prisoners incarcerated across 13 prisons did the bulk of the sewing / some famous individuals stitched choice words like *freedom* and *liberty* and *common people* / I was ashamed I had not realised that grossness immediately / though I did feel sick to my stomach after / I read about how prisoners in Jinxiang are forced to peel garlic cloves with their fingernails / until those crumble and then they have to use their teeth / who can afford domestically grown garlic / at least skin the imported bulbs yourself / the smell leaves a trail like an uncleared cache / rub your fingers across the back of a stainless steel spoon under running water / no real way to remove the odour / Gao Rong I love her work / she was born in Inner Mongolia / her family were from Shaanxi / they were forced to relocate / they used to be landowners you see / her grandmother traded craft for survival / seven children raised on needle and thread / the billionaire must have multiple hangars filled to the brim with this stuff / I could not believe my eyes / her grandparents' home and its contents reproduced in fine handiwork / floor tiles / full-scale kang / flowered quilts / peeling paint / rusty pipes / stove and wok / spatula and scoop / photographs in frames / thermoses with peonies / a pair of enamel mugs / washing machine and calendar and wall clock / mirrors and windows and doors / each fibre a memory / an infinite spool of remembrance / Do Ho Suh reconstructed his stove and toilet and sink and pipes / a red stairway floating up to a complete floor of somewhere other than here / his childhood home encased in layers of mulberry paper and charcoal-rubbed in its entirety / rubbing is a kind of loving / loving is a method of living / poetry is a way to contain time / writing is a type of fixity / artists recreate and reorder and replicate / the kitchen sink with its padded dishes / fish bones sutured on an oval plate / triptych of the bus station sign / cash strings of cryptic codes / unfired clay of the squat toilet / unfinished basin and dripless tap / not all art is beautiful but truth can make it so / find what you have to do / do it as well as you can / keep on doing it / for as long as is possible / our hands press up against the glass / make your mark / bloodless palms leave indecipherable smudges / we scroll past and past / our mosaic of faces blur into one / you cut up many flags / unpick new meanings from them / flowers are an external manifestation of sex / details are parts of the whole we cannot possibly fathom / it's nearly time / the laundry basket is overflowing / the ironing pile must be gotten through / you know you buy less when you shop on foot without a trolley / but my hands hurt from carrying the bags / remember I broke my foot recently / no poems have been accepted this week / someone dropped out of the session so you could attend for free / who would pay to talk about white privilege to a roomful of whites / Chinese waiters serve us Chinese food / no one eats the roast duck leg because it would be too messy / would anyone notice if I wrapped it in a napkin and put it in my bag for later / what goes around doesn't always come around / karma is a chameleon / I push the glistening drumstick away on the lazy susan / byebye / bye / bye

Notes:

The poem is, in part, a response to the artworks listed below:

Do Ho Suh's *My Home/s Vertical* (2014–2019), the *Hub* series, in particular *Hub: Unit G5, 23 Wenlock Road, Union Wharf, London N1 7SB, UK* (2015), *Stove, Apartment A, 348 West 22nd Street, New York, NY 10011, USA* (2013), *Toilet, Apartment A, 348 West 22nd Street, New York, NY 10011, USA* (2013), *Basin, Apartment A, 348 West 22nd Street, New York, NY 10011, USA* (2015), *Staircase III* (2010), *Rubbing/Loving Project: Seoul Home* (2013–2022), *Floor* (1997-2000), and *Who Am We? (Multicoloured)* (2000); Spike Jonze and Charlie Kaufman's *Being John Malkovich* (1999); Cornelia Parker's *Magna Carta: An Embroidery* (2015); Gao Rong's *The Static Eternity* (2012), *Level 1/2, Unit 8, Building 5, Hua Jiadi, North Village* (2010), *Station* (2011), and *Some Days Later* (2015); Lin Zhi's *Afraid of Water* (2013); Raquel Ormella's *Australia Rising #2* (2009), *New Constellation No. 1* (2013), and *Wealth for Toil No. 1* (2014).

I also make reference to Gao Rong's interview with Luise Guest on *Artist Profile*, which can be found here: https://artistprofile.com.au/gao-rong/, and to the title of the song 'Karma Chameleon' (1983) by Culture Club.

Memory Curls | ANNA JACOBSON

```
┌─────────────────┐
│  Memory Curls   │
└────────┬────────┘
         │
My │nana│ peeled apples       My │father's mother├──────┤his father│

           in           {Hungarian | aungerish} added   {Polish | poylish} added
                              sugar | tsuker                  Salt | zalts
                                                          to semalina kasha |
                                                          semolina porridge
         one

        long
                curl
                                                        │father│ says:
My │mother's├─────────────────────────┐
                                      │
         knack.                     │my│

                  │I│ lack        the Hungarian way is to add sultanas   ^
                                                                         ^
         her patience, watch apple-                                      ^
                                                                         ^
              skin streets   │curve│                                     ^
                                  out                                    ^
                      and                                                ^
                                    cloves. She │peels│ – I │carve│      ^
                   around:                                               ^
                                                                         ^
         apples            vanilla            seven cores –              ^
                                                                         ^
            sugar        cinnamon                 the Polish way

                          water
                                              On the second

                                         batch

                                              of stewed apples, sultanas

                                                          swell

                                                                full.
```

My father sits in a room alone | DŽENANA VUCIC

i.

A boy drowns in the lake. Another steps on a
landmine. Years before, a man cocks his gun.
My father sits in a room alone. The village is
empty. My father tells a joke. A man hangs himself.
The punchline is: he hangs himself from a willow.
To understand this you need to know something of
the relative weakness of the wood. Bone will break
it. My father knows. My father is a lumberjack.
Two knee surgeries. Patella, in pieces. A scar like
a bullet hole in his side. Thumb tip cut off and
sewn back on. This is just the beginning. He has
another joke about hanging. The man cannot swim.

ii.

I am tired of bean stew, of cabbage. Peppers in
vinegar. When winter comes, it's in jars. My
father and I do not speak the same language.
I am learning. Prije rata, poslije rata. Before the
war, and after. Before the war I sat in this room.
After, we were gone. Loss is too short a word
for it. Too small. How many letters in twenty-five
years. Some of us are still gone. Some of us,
still. There are no pictures on the wall. Photos
in a pile next to the tv. Papers. Dust bunnies.
Ash. Last year the forests burned. There were
floods. I didn't bring a warm enough coat.

iii.

There's always something to clean. Bathtub
slick with motor oil. Dirt. Small rocks caught
in the drain. Every light switch and door handle
smeared. I buy a new vacuum, new chemicals.
Sweep crumbs out of corners. My father's phone
plays ocean sounds. Shhhhhhhhh in the night.
My father holds scraps of metal between his
feet, wears sunglasses when he remembers. Welds
jagged edges. Makes shapes. Forgets the sunglasses.
Sparks. Eyes red, weepy. Weeping. His phone on
speaker, max volume. Shhhhhhhhh. says *sorry can
you repeat the question. Sorry I don't understand.*

iv.

Every night we watch tv. Watch the news.
Watch *Survivor,* Turkish soap operas, sitcoms,
talent shows. My father chain smokes. Fingers
black with oil. Grease. The punchline is: He
wasn't in the attic. He was in the cellar. This
is a joke about April Fool's. On Balkan *Survivor*
one host is silent the entire episode. He only
speaks on the Serb channels. There, our host
is silent. No one stops politics. Flies on fruit.
This year was a bad harvest. Everything comes
from the supermarket. Apples. A watermelon,
guillotined. Brazen peaches, wet and sloping.

v.

There's beer in the dishwasher. Rajika. Juice.
Soda, flat after opening days before. Weeks. Since
I came back my father does not drink. Back, not
home. Not yet. A woman walks a cow down
the street. Long skirt. Headscarf in the peasant
way. Later, a cow lows in a barn behind our house.
It is not the same cow, I don't think. In the war
we had a cow and then our neighbours were
killed and we had two. In the war fifteen people
lived in our house. More passed through it. We
milked the cows. Grew potatoes. Planted mines.
There's one Croat in the village. He comes to hunt.

vi.

I'm sick of not knowing what to say. This isn't a
big house. There's nowhere to go. A wasp flies
in, is lost throwing itself against glass. Thinks
better of it. One day there was a rhinoceros
beetle big as an apricot. Two days in a row I am
stung by bees. I am allergic to wasps, not bees.
My father wants to take me through the dead
orchard to the bend in the river. He wants to throw
sticks for my dog to fetch. He is allergic to tall
grass. Comes home with red welts on his ankles.
His calves. Dark like all the blood's at the surface
waiting to flood out. We need salve.

Note: after Victoria Chang's 'How Much'. The first line 'A boy drowns in the lake. Another steps on a/ landmine.' directly follows Chang's 'A boy drowns in a lake. Another opens/his head….'. I have also followed Chang's 12-line stanza structure but the poems differ significantly in theme.

from Naag Mountain | MANISHA ANJALI

I live on Minjungbal country. Tweed Shire, New South Wales. I am at the Murwillumbah-Currumbin intersection on Tomewin Road in my bone-grey Mazda 626, windows down, Mohammed Rafi on the radio. What is special about this intersection is that this sign, which points to Murwillumbah, New South Wales to the left, Currumbin, Queensland to the right, is planted among fertile green sugar cane fields. What is special about me stopping at this intersection, is that at some point, these sugar cane fields were owned by the Colonial Sugar Refining Company, the company that once owned my family.

A currawong sits on the Murwillumbah-Currumbin road sign by the sugar cane fields. I put the currawong song through my tape recorder. Criminals have made bootleg tapes of folk songs that were sung at my birth and are peddling them on the black market. Companies who owned human beings for plantation labour are still peddling their sugar at the supermarket. I put the currawong song on my fingertip. I roll the windows to the fictitious translation of tomorrow. I put tomorrow in my mouth. The first taste is betel leaf. The aftertaste is rosewater, ginger and kerosene.

Our friends live across the Tasman, on the misty horizon seen from Cape Reinga, Aotearoa. This is where two oceans meet, the lungs of the Pacific Ocean and the Tasman Sea, on an imaginary line of woven grass mats, yaqona bowls and betel nut. Our friends sit here cross-legged, no longer tethered to land or movement, for the mists are now their home.

Our friends across the Tasman are the spirits of hawkers, who stowed away to Aotearoa from Fiji, post-plantation. They peddled oranges, apples, bananas and feijoas in corroded wheelbarrows, bare feet and bare-faced, through the smoky monochrome opium mists of downtown Auckland, 1914.

When the locals protested NO HINDOOS! NO HINDOO BARROWMEN! and banned them from the streets, they lay their bananas down in the mists of the two seas.

At some point, when we crossed the Pacific Ocean to the archipelago, to Aotearoa, to Australia, at some point, we misplaced our ravanahathas, our mirrors and our lizards. We, descendants of the girmityas who still walk in the realm of the living, across many islands in the Pacific Ocean, lived in the lacuna where no dreams are seen. Our friends who live across the Tasman are dreaming our dreams for us. The instructions they receive are specific:

Walk into the film that washes ashore in your place of conception. Climb the moon when it is swollen above the cowrie shell house in the middle of the sea. Eat the jackfruit hearts that flower under the influence of the twins. Follow the folk songs of the thousand-mouthed naag into the heart of the mountain.

Next dénouement, 4th floor on the right | DAVOREN HOWARD

*This built-for purpose bird-scape
lacks scope*, I say, and you nod
approvingly, heart
openly fact-checking
its immediate vicinity, your aura
of flight-deck simplicity.
We chuckle, stabilize our vertigo,
clamp down on a bristling horizon.

From inside my changing room
I hear your call echoing
across the valley.
Simplicity makes for a smarter world
I whisper, pleased with myself, your voice
swift of wing painting halos
round a vagrant sun,
dressing skies in delicate weight.

This is no dream, I think to myself,
and you pale instantly, naked
before novelty's will to passion.
From this moment on,
minutes imitate years irritate days
as hope initiates despair,
and we continue to perch just beyond
one another's cross-fade prayers.

No Cinematic Act Could Counterfeit | LUOYANG CHEN

Confession flooded out that summer, the season of typhoons recorded in news, in memory, in that sweat-soaked scent and taste of your body, in my tongue. My mother and aunty snapped and slapped me though neither remember to this date which I doubt. But what can doubt signify except pain and guilt and *if you are like this I will abandon you I will never love you you will be better off dead?* In year two I borrowed your sci-fi book with an intention of never returning it back to you unless you return me love. In year three you kissed me once and never again. In whichever year I cannot remember I learned and memorised this line of that poem from that collection called 诗经 or *Book of Songs/Poems* and it goes [执子之手，与子偕老] which would lose all its puncture and punch when translated into English though here it is and there you go: *holding thy hand, growing old with thee.* What's missing here is Sigmund Freud, by which I mean James Strachey the translator, by which I mean MOURNING AND MELANCHOLIA.

Tonight I am filthy I am filled with nicotine. Tonight which is just like any other night you are not with me and I don't want you here either. But tonight it is the same night that I relentlessly clean my room, brush my hair, listen to 张国荣/Leslie Cheung singing 月亮代表我的心/ *The Moon Represents My Heart,* and mourn for a cinematic excellency that captures the density of loss and pain and guilt in evocative 80s dim colour and pensive melody.

> No cinematic act could counterfeit
> the hands we hold tight tonight
> in the dim Hong Kong street-
> light.

But nostalgia is poison so I actively decide to live and mourn for this moment. I walk out. I look up. There is the moon. The moon, hanging, crescent, represents my heart. And I live this moment:

my right hand reaches for
you in the dark;
        absence = more present, in which there is
no remedy no melody but pain. And it is good. It is very good.

not a drop | CATH KENNEALLY

Water On the Brain: the brutal common term
in my childhood, in fact a simple translation
— so-called hydrocephaly

my schoolmates and I once, making
a misguided adolescent descent on
the daunting 'Home for Incurables'
… to bring solace to the sick …

fetched up in a cot-room with a giant-headed
baby who haunted our dreams for years

there is water on my mind, always,
an inland sea … if I could direct my dreams, I'd
drown my enemies. I consider
ice melting, flowing back to the ocean, revealing
corpses and plane-wrecks on glaciers

hikers warned not to scale the Matterhorn
Ice freezing 2000 metres above the old ice-line
our stamping-grounds rapidly becoming swamp
our home paddocks flood-plains

'our' animals stranded on ever-shrinking islands
water reclaiming land in zones never drowned

humans perched on knolls about to go under
fingers of delta being sucked sodden
we'll all be down the drain
babies who've gone down the plughole

sea-levels go up, we go down into the dark
tsunamis outrun us, boats flake into matchsticks
fisherfolk join the fish, Moby-Dick gets his revenge

it's raining outside right now, in Adelaide
where we feel secure, except from fire; surely even that
can't get me here on the flat, amidst the safe houses
you see from the air, amicably side by side
flanked by their blue oblongs of pool

as though a ribbon of water at your door
protects you, like a totem over the lintel

the Reef is white, the ocean still turquoise
the sea will outwait us

A notice | LAURIE DUGGAN

a jet crosses the road
that splits a suburb

its sound descends
as silence did

years back, a smile
without recognition

a simile missing
a letter

On whether I subscribe to my name | ESTHER OTTAWAY

It feels like toppling, first sound a surprise –
excellence and *error* equally portended
by this avian downdraft of breath,
open lips, tongue's brink curled upward,
and just when I fear the vulnerability
of *exposed* and *entered*, the endless fall,
s gifts me wings: I'm an egret
wheeling above the wet reflective estuary,
altricial, exhilarant as estrogen,
and high on the boldness of *yes*. Esprit
and escape, spirit of fledge and pinion,
I'm at home only in flight, inability to define myself
circling and circling, so that when my claws
clatter and grab onto the *t* of tea-tree
the branch whips and bounces, everything up in the air.
Est labels me extremes: *quietest, brightest,*
esteemed, estranged, and it's a relief
to find myself, at the last, anonymous
behind the lazy accent of my culture,
the broad, bright *a* of hard yakka
and the battler, *Esta, good onya.*
Only in night's room, curled behind my collarbones,
lies like a truth that tender prayer of *her.*

our neighbours poem | ENDER BAŞKAN

our neighbours face appears above the fence – hello. our neighbours have a chat with us. our neighbours learn our names. our neighbours become our friends. our neighbours landlord thinks the market is ripe. our neighbours are told to leave. our neighbours try to buy their house at an exorbitant price to keep their kids in the school zone. our neighbours are denied. our neighbours move out. our neighbour paul calls me paul, our neighbour paul calls our other neighbour paul too. our neighbour cuts our grass, dumps the leftovers into our messy yard, leaves a bag of toys on our doorstep. our neighbours lend us a shovel we keep and lend out ourselves. our neighbours lend us a blender, give us kids clothes, and say to me – how are you? you look tired. our neighbour gives me fifty bucks to cut her grass and trim her hedges, invites me in for lemonade and tv, the tennis is on. our neighbour sings along in italian on saturday mornings and says – how are you darlin, buutifuu gerl! to my daughter. our neighbour has been in her house 55 years, raised her kids here, worked in a factory, her husband a waiter on lygon st, he died, his pin-up girl posters still hang in their garage, i use his tools, the roads were dirt when they moved in, she doesnt like our paperbark tree and says – dis tree noh gudt! too much messy! because her backyard is paved and she tires of sweeping the leaves up – ill speak to our landlord i say. our neighbours have a whatsapp group. our neighbours have dinner together on the nature strip. our neighbour is a dog sitter and breeder who yells a lot, the dogs howl into the night, she doesnt like how ive parked my car and i dont like how she speaks to me, we arent cordial. our neighbours are watching neighbours on tv. our neighbours are learning piano, its greensleeves waltzing matilda coldplay, now theyre learning trombone too, their plum tree hangs over the fence and we eat the fruit. our neighbours are home. our neighbour climbs the wobbly fence and wants to chat, tomorrow is her tenth birthday – double digits! i say. our neighbour goes away and we water their plants and when we go away they water ours. our neighbour is missing, we hear she has cancer, has chemo, we are fingers crossed. our neighbour is on the roof doing repairs and is peering into our yard, sometimes hes up there because he has a telescope. our neighbour doesnt have a name. our neighbour is in the scouts, helps me break into our house when im locked out without a shirt on, the wind slammed me out, together we finesse the window open, i give her boost, shes 9, she climbs right in. our neighbour is going camping, is packing their car, pulling a rope, truckies knot, loaded roof racks. our neighbour has chronic pain, is in and out of hospital, is often in bed. our neighbour says – if you need a babysitter im good with kids – and invites us over for dinner, her front door is always open and our daughter runs in to play dress-ups, piano, and feed the chickens. our neighbour is 26 and our daughter is 2 and they are best friends. our neighbour pours us a drink, brings us cake, introduces us to her parents. our neighbour walks into our backyard. our neighbours rhubarb plant is relocated into our veggie patch and does well. our neighbours wheelbarrow is made of plastic. our neighbours chickens get mauled by foxes and we explain this to our kid. our neighbours lend us a hiking pack and walking poles. our neighbour is a musician, gives us their cd and when theyre away, their back window is open and i climb in and borrow their guitar. our neighbours sit in their front yard, the sign of a good share house. our neighbours wife dies, he comes fishing with us, lets us cook for him, has a separate washing machine to tenderise octopus, he is 90 now and says – you like cetrioli? – and i say – yes! – not knowing what it is and he gives me four cucumbers in a plastic bag. our neighbour says – i know you like a hot chilli, heya tayk it! our neighbour hits puberty, gets a dog, the dog gets pregnant, the dog goes away to give birth. our neighbour kisses her boyfriend after school in the park and i see them. our neighbour takes long service leave, helps me cut a tree branch, shares their preferred pronouns. our neighbour lends our neighbour a mulcher and together we mulch and talk in between the searing noise. our neighbours are having a bbq, its a birthday party, they let us know beforehand. our neighbours have a trampoline in their front yard. our neighbour grows shrubs and flowers on her nature strip, everyone who comes by is impressed. our neighbours house is full of vintage textiles. our neighbour watches traffic go by, puts witches hats on the street in front of their house, washes all the cars in the neighbourhood for 30 bucks each, hes a hustler, gets a lift off me, brings me a bucket of m&ms, says – nice day! – says – you car look dirty! says – you work late today!? – says – you bring me some of that turkish bread, ok!? – our neighbour drives an uber he keeps immaculately clean. our neighbour says – what can you do i no complain! our neighbour asks me to be a reference for her visa application. our neighbour has loud sex. our neighbour has raucous parties, drum n bass from midday friday till sunday afternoon. our neighbour runs down the stairwell without saying hi, is an overworked teacher. our neighbour waters their balcony plants and it dribbles onto my head as i hang the clothes. our neighbour doesnt bring their bins in. our neighbours waters break. our neighbours pipes burst. our neighbour brings our bins in. our neighbour parks in our carspot. our neighbour leaves boxes of cosmetics on the footpath and we take some body oil. our neighbours are ripping bongs, are gaming, are squatters. our neighbour owns our house, subdivided and build a fortress next-door. our neighbour has two cars, a lambikini and a commodore, takes me for a ride in the commodore to his warehouse full of pinball machines and a '57 Chevy to find spare keys in metal drawers after a gust of wind locks me out. our neighbour pours his heart out to me in the car, says – my lifes gone to shit bro, my dad died, my mum died, my woman betrayed me – he misses his mum, i put my hand on his shoulder, he has his exs stuff in garbage bags in the back seat, he talks fast, drives reckless, likes speed. our neighbour doesnt respond to our texts, were having a party and want his blessing, later his family arrive dressed in black. our neighbours are buddhist monks, have a high brick fence. our neighbours stop to chat when we sit on our front lawn. our neighbours give us lemons. our neighbour lets me into her house after ive locked myself out, has many erotic sculptures, gives me tea and biscuits before i jump the fence. our neighbour has lived here 57 years, is deaf, we crank the music higher. our neighbour was my housemate who moved out to move in with her boyfriend a few doors down. our neighbours and i make ice cream. our neighbours sister has just moved to melbourne. our neighbours sister wants to come over for a drink. our neighbours sister knocks on the door and i open it, i say – hello, come in, do you want a drink? our neighbour has a garage sale and i buy their shirt. our neighbour finds a scrunched-up piece of paper hurled over the fence by our other neighbour that reads – have a good party, enjoy yourselves, enjoy your youth, fuck everything that moves!!! our neighbour is a widow whose husband taught my mum at school. our neighbour stands outside and watches the street go by, sometimes he carries home a slab of VB on his shoulder. our neighbour has a baby, has another baby, has a third baby. our neighbour has a sign on their fence that reads – no to inappropriate developments. our neighbour tests the market, sells their house, buys their house, rents their house, renovates their house, demolishes their house, develops the land, builds units, sells the units, keeps one for themselves. our neighbour makes the money. our neighbour bangs on the floorboards when i play music. our neighbour smiles her golden tooth. our neighbour stays up late smoking on their balcony. our neighbour is a bakery. our neighbour takes in the delivery guy quickly. our neighbour is a police station. our neighbour is a house of students. our neighbour is my best friend now. our neighbour and i kiss after pot-luck dinner. our neighbour and i play soccer together, she puts her hand on my thigh in the back of a taxi, wants to sleep in my bed tonight. our neighbour offers me a ciggie, pours us some wine. our neighbour sleeps in my bed, lays in it while i make breakfast, has a boyfriend overseas, is in the shower, is on my mind, walks out wet. our neighbour is a doctor. our neighbour doesnt know that i jumped the fence to get my ball and their dog bit me. our neighbour borrows our surfboard. our neighbour becomes leader of the greens. our neighbour is an electrician, calls me boy. our neighbour knocks on the door to play with me and my mum says no, probably because hes a bit older and rides a bmx with a low seat and has a rats tail. our neighbours dont share a fence with us. our neighbours house smells like cigarettes, like curry, like roast, like a chip shop. our neighbours are celebrating ramadan and the street is full of cars. our neighbour collects triumph cars in their yard. our neighbours are greek. our neighbours are macedonian, we are not, but my parents say we understand one another anyway. our neighbours have me over, give me lifts to school, their daughter is a year older than me and i love her. our neighbours let me jump the fence and play footy cricket soccer and basketball, their grandma lives with them, they give me yum lebanese food, we make tapes on their stereo, throw water bombs. our neighbours dad works night shift in the tyre factory so we gotta be quiet. our neighbour jump starts our car. our neighbour waves to us. our neighbour brings over clothes when i am born. our neighbours say hello.

Overheated | AMY CRUTCHFIELD

Back from the ashes like a phoenix
company. Promises not worth the paper.
The regulator sighs, it's overheated.

They say accounts because
everyone recalls it differently.
There is no auditor.

Cash is taught by insolvency.
When the buck stops
we are what we consent to.

Subordination is a common arrangement.
In a liquidation we ask
whose promise was bigger?

A Passage Through | ANGELA GARDNER

                                        it looks hopeless
on the flip: the forest, the hurled world overhead
its falling horizon clearly inserted beyond immaculate.
Under the derelict sky a dynamo skews through
landscape sharpening the sun. I breathe a nowhereness
familiarity removed. In the lost figure of myself
we are marked as random and excessive. This is not
how you look at a lake.
                              You were the nearest
to real in my life. Now volatile currents haze the wind,
blackened columns replace eucalypts and intermittent
chemical-flare enters our breathing. The gaze's touch
is distraught over charred ground, body-clutter,
animal truth. We fight against corrosion, silt tongues
learning a swallowed language. It is a bleak corridor
lined with condolence.
                              And here's the thing
sometimes you can't read a passage through for
creeping erasure, economic grasping, ourselves.
Mirrors fold, hollow against many enclosures, as we look
elsewhere for an exit. Emotion, concealed maybe.
A place only in my mind, where still there is an idea
of returning.

Phalaris / Perennial | THOM SULLIVAN

the tedder in its season :
the tractor in the last light
that goes on circling :
working the phalaris :
turning back along
its line : my father is there
among them : among those
men who stand in the
twilight : with the mud
of acres on their hands :
a glint of quartz dust :
who have smelled the must
of grasses as they walk back
through nightfall : easing
their bodies over fences :
feeling the tension of
wires with expert hands :
if i walk out to meet him
some night : with the last
light over my shoulder
like a past : like a promise :
or i surprise some quail
that darts up & merges
with the hour : with the
texture of grasses as they
jostle : unspoked : if you
stand there : how long will
you stand there : have you
stood there : even now :

Please stop talking about ancient Rome | NATHAN CURNOW

it's not as interesting as ancient Rome—
how the slave girl filled the water clock,
how the scribe mixed ink for the scroll.
You just love the big names, their victories
and defeats. Destiny, legacy. Yeah, I get it,
you're talking about yourself. Even Caesar
had to come home sometimes, and then
they heard about it. Ugh. The rhetoric.
What's a man to become without lending
from the big man library? Love it enough
and you'll burn it. You'll conspire to save
the republic. Try flea-treating the dog,
taking up those pants or catching the bus
to school council. Vote for what's required
beyond personal repute. Don't push
for columns in the quadrangle or
a gravity-fed aqueduct. Find your glory
in little things. Discover greatness there.
Who collected the towels at the bathhouse?
Who fell in love on campaign in Gaul?
Tell me of a road that led nowhere.
And how did they treat their horses?
Were peacocks allowed in the temple
or were they shooed out every morning?
I'll meet you on the steps. Imagine,
your only battle is to age and age well,
that character is a fortune to pass along
and your heir is the entire world—the slave,
the scribe, an empire, that one day has to fall.
Why can't you love the Autumn fog
that settles long and low?

pork lullaby | PANDA WONG

If you feed me garbage, / I will sing a song of garbage.
—'Pig Song' by Margaret Atwood

     to be a pig   is to know the word *crush*
   Miss Piggy's eternally unrequited crush on
emotionally unavailable Kermit
neither cast ye your pearls before swine
   lest they trample them under their feet (Matthew 7:6)
      common cause of neonatal piggy death—
       sows rolling over in their sleep,
long histories of breeding for feeding means
  that like cliffside mansions in the Anthropocene
   their organs are prone to
       collapse.
    speaking of organs,
   how fast do you think
     those little ham hock hearts were beating
  when those two wild hogs mugged hip-shaking
hips-don't-lie Shakira in a public park?
     speaking of hearts,
  i cut open a pig heart in year five biology
   its pinkness its pipes its precious parts
   the closest to ours out of every living thing in the world.
       speaking of the world,
   i am thinking abt how pigs see it,
  dichromatic vision pouring out from their eyes
solidifying objects as pure colour
   for example— they may see the
    blue of the sky as wide expanse

        but not any clouds or rainbows
     it may hold.
   well-known industry fact— stress before
slaughter can make pig flesh
        D F   D
        (Dark! Firm! Dry!)
         an AI pig farm in China
      plays ambient mix on loop
       to captive porcine audience,
     to oink-oink-optimise
   how their bodies feel
     against our teeth.
      in opposition to its name, tenderising
     is a brutal act who else has ever seen
  a tenderiser & thought *medieval torture device?*
     we are always
       oink-oink-optimising
        our own tender meat—
  i am the same age as the word *biohacking,*
have submitted myself to
   the indignities of Pilates
   sheet masks made from boiled bones
     &   first dates with men
     who swore by intermittent fasting.
   lifestyle guru gives himself
  resveratrol-induced shits in the pursuit of endurance,
something spiritual abt

shitting yourself towards transcendence,
                 the   slop-slop-sublime.
         i am watching a video of Lotus,
                  piggy sweetie rescued
      from a life as dog bait,
   she carefully gathers flowers
to decorate her home
       & in this way   the poem
            can be a pig sty.
   at a farm animal sanctuary,
  i am   learning abt
     how we have made pigs
       pink out of a preference for
           light-skinned meat &
              how being under the sky & the sun
    burns their skin to   a bacon crisp.
their bodies are   mighty meaty odes to   multitasking,
       a dead pig is
        beating ham
          sticky heart
           brined glue
        but   an alive pig
         roots in the soil
       turning it over
      with its snout
         softening the ground
             is this   a hymn

Portmanteau | JAYE KRANZ

noun, figurative: a word formed by blending sounds from two or more distinct words and combining their meanings; also a transitive verb

Remember the stag
    you felt sure you saw in halflight

wondering who would want to shoot it
    broadside or quartering away

when all it wanted was to walk here
      among the applehalves

    my dog at the open door nosing zephyrs
    wresting warm bodies from the cold

& you might not believe in ghosts
    as if we can all agree on what exists

    between a clear night & this dew
      between fate & what was only

staying in motion,
    between coming closer

      felling a tree
          patience

      & what was just
        the applesfalling.

What is the distance
    between the orangeseed we planted

      & the grapefruit that grew there;
between you handing me the peeledripe fruit

        & me wondering if the tree still lives, still sways
           in that garden

      that seemed to garden forever.
There seemed to me only three gardens then:

mine, yours & the one you'd take me to,
    bags of stale bread

to feed the ducks, readymade for the lovers, the gardenlovers
    the ducks, the ducklovers

      & those who would soon
        breakapart—

whoever made the bags having no idea
stale bread was your bread of choice, the bread you broke most

leaving loaves on your countertops
    until they staled.

As if we remember the same things
or the same things remember us

I remember some of you—
    the way you drove in a thunderstorm

      like we'd washaway;
the way you traced your tools broad & black on the shed wall

to return them to their outlines.
 But I never understood why, just after you died

you visited my friend but not me,
  though you came once

stood on the porch outside my bedroom window
to teach me a mnemonic

 for the order of planets,
  unbothered that Pluto had ceased to be

the *'P'* in your acrostic,
 having proved itself unable—or unwilling?—

to be set apart
 to clear its regions of neighbouring bodies.

 I move with Pluto, now
& the halflight things

portmanteaus in porchlight
 flicking in

& out
 with the light sensors,

 seen there in that tiny age
  half-remembered, half-forgotten

washed out by the full tilt of the sun.

Reception Theory or How to Sit in an Office Chair
| AUTUMN ROYAL

'What I hide by my language, my body utters.'
—Roland Barthes

Before the telephone rings again we should touch
on the things that make her human in combination
with her ill-fitting clothes—a skirt too tight
around the waist and the jumper so loose the sleeves
drag along the tiled floor—the lamb she nurses
in her lap is surely a convincing marker that she
is what one would call a person and should be held—
in the office chair—as the individual who
owns the voice providing the etiquette of greeting
other people with a warm and welcoming *hello*—
pronounced clearly and with appropriate volume.
Water drips into an empty bucket as she inhales air
and exhales longing for the burden of disappointing
someone very much like herself. A patron enters
the building, crushing leaves underfoot. Her wet-haired
willingness shifts into the lamb's body—she returns
to the field, on her back and rustic—the telephone rings.

The record player | STUART BARNES

(With a nod to Marianne Moore's 'The Fish')

       dins:
   Cocteau Twins'
'Frou-frou Foxes in Midsummer Fires'
phosphoresces: tripwires
    invisible to me (*Silly*

       String?
   Silly…) spring
stillness into him. I scratch his ass
-essment ('*Heaven or Las*
    Vegas: best wall of sound album.'):

       '*The*
   Head on the
Door echoes in oh! six different ways.'
(If only all Mondays
    were this uncomplicated.) A

       car
   plays bizarre
scales: brilliance spills into the bedroom:
a vase of dried Scotch broom
    prances on the mantel, wooden

       fish
   score their wish:
gold glitter skitters on the water
unrolled by the daughter
    of Nereus and Doris who

                              peers

                    over spears,
dolphins and seals at these gordian
reels. The accordion
              in the corner squawks discordant

                              as
                  Junior's jazz
jerks into the night. Darkness larks. We
kiss, still hopeful, still free,
              still post-punks listening for your

                              track's
                  bliss. Dead wax
teases the needle: our lullaby

buds. We'll sleep thigh to thigh,
              DJ, poet, tuning the moon.

Note: Herman "Junior" Cook was a hard bop tenor saxophone player.

from *Repetend* ('a novel's a relaxing thought') | *STUART COOKE*

Óvalo literario, la circularidad de la presencia, inflexión que se apaga en el acto que se consuma…

—DAVID HUERTA

a novel's a relaxing thought, but the words from whatever mouth you open will crumble to dust a novella's a rel
billowing clouds of dust cover Beijing, cover Brisbane billowing clouds of dust cover Beijing, cover Meanjin billo
the land's coated with the blood of your lungs the land's coated with the blood of your longes the land's coated
under the tarmac it's clammy and fetid under the tarmacadam it's clammy and fetid under McAdam's tar it's cla
but East Sydney glistens like preserved cassette but East Sydney glistens like a pre-served car set but East Sydney
Perhaps the problem isn't my solipsism, then perhaps the problema isn't my solipsism, then perhaps the próblē
but rather its impossibility, because buten rather its impossibility, because būtan rather its impossibility, because
I will always lose myself in others, simultaneou~   ~o myself in others, simultaneously I will always
or one at a time, over stretches of time or   of time or one at a time, over stretches of
others knit time together others knit tin   'er others knit time together others knit
but foreclose the granular snippets but .   t foreclose the granular snippets but for
watch them scatter into dust watch them .   .catter into dust watch them scatter into d

At your wake, in a modest, weatherboard home at your wake, in a modest, weatherboard home at your wacu, in
they drape scorched flowers over the weeping they drape scorched floures over the weeping they drape scorched
machine of my voice, and a chorus machine of my voiz, and a chorus machine of vakti, and a chorus machine of
steams up from the core. Dialogue's drizzled steams up from the core. Die, a log's drizzly steams up from the co
over a retina charcuterie over a rented shark ute, hairy over rented char, cute & hairy oval retinas & shark uteri o
rhymes are plugs, I curl my toes rhymes are plugges, I curl my toes rhymes are plove, I curl my toes rhymes are
in your docile rug, carbon couples in your docile rọgg, carbon couples in your docile rǫgg, carbon couples in you

Reverse Horse Poem | TOBY FITCH

for Frankie

Which direction is the horse walking for you? you asked, flashing your phone at me while concealing the text of the meme, and I immediately doubted what I was seeing, thinking that if I was seeing the black and white horse walking backwards, to the right on screen, I was likely in the wrong side of my brain, because I'd been feeling wrong for over two years, having not written more poems in that time than I could count on one hand—preferably the left, to spite my right-handedness and uphold a belief that what I've been told about lefties being the more creative is right—but in that moment I couldn't see the horse walking forwards, to the left on screen, no matter how hard I willed it—like coercing your eyes to see the animal hiding in a Magic Eye stereogram, which never works when you force it, and you know you just need to unclench and it'll come, but I couldn't—so I said *Backwards*, hoping this might prove me to be the imaginative type I'd lately failed to be, and then you read out the text of the meme: *If you see the horse walking forward you're left-brained, and if you see the horse walking backward you're right-brained*, and I thought, of course I'm fucking right-brained, that explains why I can't write poems anymore, and then you said *I'm backwards too*, and read further, *If you're mostly analytical and methodical in your thinking, the theory says that you're left-brained, and if you tend to be more creative or artistic, you're right-brained*, and then I—recalling the last time I'd played a binary game like this and fallen on the analytical side of things—insisted, though not quite endearingly enough, *That's not us, we're messy*, to which you bridled, *No that's right*, that I was wrong, and then we sat in silence long enough for me to realign my understanding of which hemisphere is which, and what side of the binary thinking I should like to fall on, kind of unwinding my second guessing of it all, and soon I thought of how you, a skilled rider, know intimately the various complex patterns of leg movements a horse's brain instinctively initiates to walk, trot or canter, and how much you'd loved returning to horse riding, and how naturally after many years on the two trail rides I bought you for your birthday, or birthdays, one from pre-Covid times that had seen the booking stagnate due to floods, fires and plague, and one for your current birthday, trail rides that eventually had me grappling as a fledgling for a total of five hours on two separate, immense and ripped creatures moving beneath me, clip-clopping and trotting from muscle memory, one of whom, Snoop Dogg, the first and larger of the two, after we'd traversed a hillside clearing came to an abrupt halt at the start of a new bush trail because a huge stag had appeared at the same time a train was thundering across the ridge, reared, quickly reversed himself and cantered me back across the top of the clearing while, behind us, you and your horse left our guide in a bog to round up Snoop Dogg before I could fall off ingloriously, back into the present day which galloped away and I thought nothing more of my doublethink until much later, after midnight, in the shower when something coalesced in my form as I did the little physio exercises that I'd been repeating for a few weeks to correct the last few years of favouring the left side of my body due to some nasty arthritis in my right big toe, even though my left big toe had had the more traumatic history with a basketball injury that saw its entire nail removed and a poem concocted to prove it, and so now that my right side was reawakening to its unconscious role in the whole functioning of my meat and bones, and our kids at six and eight years old still don't care to tell their left hands from their right and I've given up teaching them how to remember which is which as it doesn't matter, it dawned on me that I could write this poem, my fourth new poem in four days, as you sleep beside me perhaps dreaming of a Pegasus, and keep riding it until dawn if necessary, and it is, because my brain's been doing what I'd hoped it would be doing all along, as it understands that you can't write a poem without being an animal in its non-binary body.

Review | DAVID STAVANGER

Real estate agent sends me a new lease || with a larger increase than prior years || I suggest a halfway place || where we can meet in the middle || of their increased costs || servicing a Lexus || branded gym gear || and my decreasing faith || in secure future housing || the outsourcing of angels || the lease has both landlords listed || investment couple || so I look them up online || they're on a podcast || talking about buying 9 properties || in 15 months || in that same period || I ate approximately 51 Coles croissants || have much gravitas to show for it || one of their websites is about building empires || selling things people want to buy || like ads for clients || anything platinum || conceptual coins || and the biggest life lessons || that it's not easy to turnaround a cruise ship || that there's a good reason || niche rhymes with rich || which it doesn't || but who am I to correct || he provides off-shore staffing solutions || I find a post of theirs on socials || about passing government taxes onto tenants || which makes it sound like a baton || as if we're in the same race || as if we're both really living || under the same roof || and I will get to cross the line || between us || their main childhood recollection || seems to be about imported products || lessons learnt in their twenties || that a party is all about the numbers || and money never gets old || I am getting older || prefer small gatherings || the main thing I learnt in my twenties || is that people like them || will always take the last beer || from your fridge

Snow Burial | CATH DRAKE

My friend, you once told me if you ever get to ninety
you'll go to a frozen country and lie down naked

on the snow to die. If you're serious, I'd ask
to come with you. We'd talk all the way

about what we childless people do and how
you once helped your mum prepare for an operation

by getting up at four to disinfect her whole body.
I'd be a sheet of emotion, a weather front

and you'd say *I'm fine* as you always do
even when you aren't, yet this time you'd show me

how fragile that feels. I'd remember all those times
you threw a blanket over me by just talking.

I'd have made you a thin sprawling silk cloak
in red-purple-blue-yellow sewn with hot country flowers

from home: Swan River Daisies, spider orchids, wattles
and I'd lift it, billowing over your head, over

your congested body and would you let me
brush your hair and pin in pink and white everlastings?

Then, for both of us, I'd go over everything from the start –
how far we've come, and we'd laugh like the woods.

As you close your eyes, I'd say, *It's alright, I don't need you
to mirror me anymore,* Debussy bursting from a tiny speaker

and that's when a hawk would dip close to the earth
and give you a last look at the spectacular.

Still life in brown | ALI JANE SMITH

You're not waiting as it crosses earth, bark, rock, you're not waiting as it overtakes the weathered concrete, hardwood sleepers, runs its fruiting body across the ground in pleated skirts the tea colour of a fancy silk organza, it arrives, it was there all along, it hasn't finished.

Juan Gris makes a collage *Flowers* the colour of clay that can become a dish or a flower or a pipe, wet earth changed to a sexy assemblage of stems and bowls. Gertrude Stein buys it, the war hasn't even started, she wants to help him out, they're friends, and it's a good picture, as a picture and as something to look at with your mind when you're far away doing a horrible duty instead of enjoying talk and pipes and pictures, a bowl of something and a rose that might have been pink or flame gold but left to itself turns the colour of parchment and gets like thin parchment to touch, but don't touch it, it's not a rose or parchment, it's wallpaper, and it's on the wall at home, not here in the ambulance in the war.

I've never felt more like a wildebeest, walking with other wildebeest, so many of us, thinking about the terrain and each other, what we'll eat and what wants to eat us, kicking out for joy or to keep off a predator, we are a sign of the season and we read the signs of the seasons.

You cut back the flowers of friendship, cut the wallpaper into the shape of a rose, you're not waiting, you barely think of what will happen, it's not like growing flowers climbing, budding, bursting, seeding, parching, curling, dropping, cut them back to grow fresh bright stems and stamens, petals, creased and fluttering. You cut shapes and bring them to one another, forms burst like spores taking things further than you've been before.

Surely | MELINDA BUFTON

In the studio I think of excess and my own propensity to be always leaving *because where to?*

What happened was this –

While my nose twitched with the lit 2067AD candle (Dr. Cooper special edition)

ahead tilted sideways

I am reading an interview with Twyla Tharp, that interesting mojo

coming up to mingle with my thoughts re everlasting art, and

the *smartphone view* of this has paginated the words 'commissioned' three

Times in a row on the left *margin*. It's seemingly a typo, but no because

it's a quote. Each time different. Three times a charm. This simultaneous shadow

though

shifts across my peripheral. Aha. You colourless beauty I see you now my anima my

slippery whisp.

My conspirator and pursed sign.

Synesthesia through Binoculars
(or When I thought I saw the Green Comet but it Was
Only a Shooting Star) | SHEY MARQUE

We took off beach-side to escape the trees
the air warm and doughy, the foretelling
swelling in our lungs like leavening bread.
We were circling beneath the hunter
when I became distracted by your face—
how it held all the light of a street lamp
one second, shadowless, nothing to declare,
and a loose hound the next, the angled eye.
In the clearing we stood heads tilted back
gaping at the comet's gas trail sweeping
its cold-eyed arc across the sky. The ice
clatter of emerald against my teeth,
a trace of mint in that one fine moment
you opened and swallowed it, tail and all.

The Tableland Hour | ASHLEY HAYWOOD

1.
        Distant back-
                burn
                muffles
long conversation
between
        snowy mountains.
        Words hang on the wind-wearers
            like bats in the back of mind.
            Who's there?

        Who scratches
        around bones
            stuck
        between   limestone teeth?

2.

        A murmur of starlings
        mid-air
                rolls   as one tongue
                over   the   slow   wet   grass—
                wings cut
                            the soft

palate of sky
as I scratch
        around for wool
        like a rat

and I worry
and I worry—

        the flock turns
        like chin and cheek
                an eyelid half-interested—

                what have I done
                what haven't I done?

3.

On a long walk away from away
the hour arrives on all fours
        with bundles of night

        on its back.
        What is in the night
                emptying out? Am I
                -

                -            *echo*
        made of spare parts
        for the bodies
        to come? Ears prick.
        -

        -

        -

        -

I lay awake in the company of lambs
engineered to say nothing

        forget.
        I'll be gone by morning.

Tender | FELICITY PLUNKETT

Let me be tender. Let me soften
my hold. Give up topiary
and dogma. Let me be tender

as light – dark-breaking to dusk
glisk – and water – enough to nourish
not burn, swamp. Let me be

tender, calm. Let me loosen harm
from my body, the garden,
the whole world's yard. Let me

be tender enough to leave
untended what blossoms without
my zealous hand, my watering-can. Let

me be tender, the way a plant ally
floats close over the footpath,
giving itself, balm. Let me be tender:

mother of chamomile, champion
of lavender, whorl and corolla
of a daughter's laughter. Let me be

tender, a gentle evictor
of what scoffs basil at night, reduces
to skeleton anyone's freedom. Let me

be tender as a nurse among nurses,
from axil to bract, quiet
on my feet, a pact to be attentive. Let

me honour the trace of her cells
forever in my tissues, blood. And to all
that heals, let me be tender.

Terminal 1: Aer Lingus | DAVID PRATER

"A dictionary of shelter"
– JOHN TRANTER, 'LUFTHANSA'

Flying over violet-crumble seas, eyes bulging as the rock
rushes by (a sense of stained-glass futures, a fatal diorama
I'm descending through time with an airman's precision—
the shroud of a cloud's lop-sided laptop strata slips a little
as I glimpse the patchwork, or a field, or a metaphor (and
bank (becoming faintly religious—see the world's correction
while my references slide: taking apart the allusion of mist
with the probability of coffee (or, at least, "creamer"—o-or
you, passively declaring *the card does not want to be tapped* (smile
as you have been trained, brave crew! Your make-up that is
almost always applied too thickly, in Limerick for example,
a good time always to be had up there (yr unknown hands
of analogue, orange nail-polish, you phrased yr Gaelic lines
to a perfectly polished post-landing *denouement*, spelling
Humanism, or was it the pilot, nailing his 180 like a motto
whispered to the Shannon runway? Leaning to the far side

        (—awww, my nearest exit *was* behind me!

of the sky, an absentee landlord in hot pursuit. That the sun
has a lens flare, or some deliberate, obscured designer's flaw
is not worth contemplating at this height. It's your old flame.
And there to meet you by the car-hire desk, her hair: grey
shakes in your wake (wait—never mind, can you navigate it?
The car-hire parking area's squashed cigarette-butt promises
speak their way into the vehicle, while you punch its screen
its prior agreements about alcohol-free beers (stumble back
to a crowded cafe, somewhere, perchance to dream a drink
trolley, the zeitgeist clinging to all the beards like raindrops
a smudge of toothpaste in your reflection, in every porthole

blitzes of twisted shandy (wake: order a no-name lemonade
and note that your ancestors grew no taller than this ceiling.
No, there's mime in the genealogy centre, or was it Katharina
sleeping on the tight ship whose mistress she is, sir? Captain
lifts a hiking trail brieflet from a plastic display case on a wall
explaining Dysert O'Dea Castle & Environs as if 't were a lake
as (no time for maudlin, no maiden—you send it elsewhere
under bridges where a river moves fast (& floating in it, stars.

Note: The first and last words of each line in this poem (apart from the indented line) also appear in John Tranter's poem 'Lufthansa'.

The time traveler promises it all | RORY GREEN

If there is still a future then we are a part of it.
And there we choose names that follow our feelings: I say
nice to meet you, I'm Yearning, and you say hi Yearning
I'm Hopeful. All creatures do this, as we are only creatures too.
The tetchy magpie, the hurried ants, the curious ibis.
In the future language is a park we spend the day in.
When we find ourselves in silence, the future grows new
words to help us, words for how the back of your hand feels
and words for the look between us when last drink
becomes second-last and then third-last. In the future
we are reunited with the opportunities we passed up
which tilt their head to the sun and say go on then.
In the future we dress the city in mirrors and run
a small but efficient economy of glances. In the future
we've invented ways of measuring days that feel like minutes,
ways of touching that feel like a good year. I know we've earnt this
because I lived it. Just wait, we are a part of it.

Thinking in the Heat Wave About Clothes, Coins, Yearning, Flying Foxes and What I Cannot Escape | JILL JONES

every person you love
   you lose

even the dictionary
dithers over its verbs
   consume or obsess
fixate or possess

then there's the
   re-naming
what is now a coin

not gold or silver
not copper or nickel
   a screen swipe
or blockchain

who gets to keep their clothes
   who dies with
their clothes

we leave them in piles
   by old rivers

everything you love
you lose
   even the air has not
escaped us

maybe it will

yearning isn't nature
    it's where we were lost

in the cracks weeds grow
into the cracks
    the shades go

flying foxes fall
    from a hot sky

what can you slip
    into a pocket

torn-up stanzas

Three Days and Six Years | KERRY GREER

I.
You've arrived back from outer space.
You're holding an apple that I brought for you
to eat on the drive home. I can see from your face
that you've seen the moon
up close. But you're not telling me about that.
You're telling me about the space suit,
how it made you sweat. How it took three days
to reach the moon—three days away, away,
away. I've researched all of this. I already know,
but I let you speak because—
How your voice is lovely after all these days.
Your profile as you smile.
I want the gaps, the silence, where you might
look out the window, let the moon ride in the car
between us, a great glowing jar
of unreality. And cold too, at first, to the skin,
where the real world draws its borders.

Of course, they're not really days, you say.
There is no change from light to dark,
no twilight zone, no grey. Just units of 24, and 24,
and 24. Relics, arbitrary blocks. After a time,
I would have adapted to Total Dark—to endless Time.

Later, you carry your suitcase upstairs
and lay it flat on the bed, enter the code for the lock,
which surely you used out of habit,
not from fear of theft by fellow elite
human beings selected for the journey.
It almost feels like I never left, you say.

I was here all along, passing through these invisible hours
like virtual reality, like hide-and-seek
with my eyes open.

II.

After we kiss
and remember
each other,
I take your laundry, the days of sweat,
to the washing machine while you shower.
The water cold then hot then steam across
the mirror, when I walk in to find you—

III.

No, you definitely left, I say.
I lived out the waiting.
I watched the sky in black and light,
felt the angles of the hours,
hoped the speck of you would return
soon. It seemed like years down here,
especially in the daytime
when the moon disappeared,
and it was hard to believe in either of you.
I read books. I researched near-death experiences.
I passed the time the only way I could.

IV.

All of this is imaginary.
You're not coming back.
I keep your unwashed clothes
sealed inside a zip-lock bag.

I eat the apple for you,
imagining what you would say
as you sit in the passenger seat.
I drive you everywhere I go,
I daydream for you, watch you
watching life passing by
just beyond the glass.

V.

I want to take my eyes off the road
to look at you. Did you dream in daylight?
I ask. But you are silent, somewhere far away
in thought. Not everybody could adapt, I say.
Some of us would lose our minds in the space
between grief and death, the not-knowing
when it ends or when life begins again—

VI.

Before I clear the steam, I see you.
If I wait long enough, you wait too.
Like a game. Like virtual reality.

Touch free wash | STEPHANIE POWELL

An un-beautiful place looked at differently, luminant in neon and the feeling of God watching the CCTV. The Servo. Tonight, capturing me in depression clothing and sandals in winter, I have come for the empty calories and to read newspaper headlines. Vehicles queue for the automated carwash, 2 *washes 4 20 bucks*. I am only looking out the window at my other body outside the glass, seeing it standing on the threshing floor. The air is red with mist and coloured light. I close my eyes and each sound is its own machine. The automatic doors open and close and the traffic is a tide that never touches. Sonia tells Uncle Vanya, *we must go on living*. I must stay upright a little longer, until the water cures or kills me.

Citation: Anton Pavlovich Chekhov, from Russian to English translation of *Uncle Vanya*, 1897. Translation: Elisaveta Fen (Lydia Jiburtovich-Jackson), Penguin Classics; Penguin Classic edition, 1959.

Unbalancing | HAZEL SMITH

It was one of those weeks when you think the calamities can't pile up anymore, until they do. Every day boasted a number, but I seemed to be counting down to my death. Every hour brought a throw of the dice that didn't fall my way. It was a game, punishable in the most painful manner.

On the first day, a man with wild hair and a beard approached me in the street. He said, 'you have to get married immediately, if you don't there will be irreversible consequences for you and everyone you love'. I said, 'I don't have anyone in mind, can't we go a little slower?' He said no, push the accelerator down, it has to be done now. Make a list. He claimed to work for the government.

The next day, a man called me and said that someone we both knew was taking me to court for defamation. His voice was low and muffled, so I didn't catch every word. But worse, I couldn't remember what I had said or understand why it had caused such offence. I could deny it, but that wouldn't necessarily convince him. I could hang up because maybe it was a scam. I kept trying to recall what I had said, there was even a part of me that actually believed him. I started to wonder about leaving the country, but it was then I was told that the borders were closing.

After that three men came to the door and said they were taking away my fridge. No explanation. I told them I couldn't live without it, but they said it had to go and promised that sometime in the near future they would bring me a new one. They were extremely evasive about the replacement which made me realise there wasn't one. The food was all on the counter and I knew it would soon start to rot. Just when it seemed as if that was my quota of bad fortune, my publisher rang me up to say he wouldn't be publishing my book. He seemed very unsure why, his voice was faintly tinged with regret but painted with the irreversible.

***

she has lived a life of unbalances

      to be weightless is the ultimate grounding or so she believes

astronauts return to earth hungry for outer space

      time zones bloom asymmetrically, a footstep tastes of champagne.

each morning brings a bag of tremors and a blessing

    as the dawn sprays its cool invective

flow is pegged on flight lines

      do not talk to me, you will disturb this poetic chattering

she has always been passionate about her own interiority

      every misshapen nook, every slanting floor

    in the real world adults are reading newspapers, outraged by violation

let's celebrate the squint, the limp, the suspended and the halting

a moment of composure opens like a lily, heroically out of control

    no life can be paraphrased, every summation falls precipitously short

verticals collapse as they leave the 3D landing site

    a sense of calm, a twisted sky, precede the penultimate feast

***

Advice is useful: it allows you to do the opposite.

The true revolution will come when people say what they mean.

He kept insisting it was a paradox, as if that was an explanation.

When each day is similar, life feels more secure, but secure spells monotonous.

Usually, the answers she received seemed to belong to a different question.

Everyone's sensitivity to risk is different: one person's comfort zone is another's anxiety trip.

A woman who was already pregnant conceived another child. Talk about the odds, talk about redundancy.

Should you tear down a tree because it would improve your neighbour's view?

Should you spill a secret to reveal a troubling root?

Thoughts were only thoughts until you acted on them but most of the time you didn't.

Guilt is brutal and untameable.

The satisfactions cancel out the hungers.

Somehow, he never had the conversation he wanted to have.

Somehow, you never wrote the book you longed to write or thought you could.

When the ending came, she felt it must be her fault. She had ruined lives. She should have acted differently. They told her the fallout had nothing to do with her, but the sadness trailed behind her, the shame would never stop. She was convinced, beyond all reasoning, of her culpability.

Under Fang | CHRIS ANDREWS

Day my colour-bound myopia,
before you go can I just say how
claret leaves cut puzzles in the blue
and what the skywriter hearted there
was anybody's progressive guess.
Day the only place for us to park
our demountable utopia,
don't slip away like a timid guest
before I can say just how you go.

Another brilliant day gone missing
the never-yet-assembled fragments,
with nothing to guide me but the ghost
of a pattern: net trap set to catch
the matter that could make a part whole.
Rumbly bins, Venus dipping to kiss
lichen-crusted tiles, and here you are:
dusk my shot of myalgia my
shadow-flooded topiary maze.

It might be true, what my brother says:
I like to aim low. My ambition:
to remain an opsimath. Success:
not having quite given up just yet.
But I stand under a blown street lamp.
It's Alphard, so my phone-eye tells me,
at the far end of the starlight thread.
Somebody watching under you, Fang.
Deep sky night my ache my opiate.

Unholy Verses | SARA M SALEH

How the seas emptied of salt
And the tides swelled
And the pipelines built
And the gas pumped
And the forests logged
And the fisheries depleted
And the reef bleached
And the mountains landslided
And the bees starved
And the stars absconded
And the sky broke open
And the planet tuberculated
And the corporations monetised
And the surveillance digitised
And the protestors fined
And the people calloused
And the laws ossified
And the women paid first
And the bodies of earth testified against us.

An Urn of Ash & Bees | ION CORCOS

White blossoms sprout not long after the last snow melts. On a chimney, a rock pigeon turns, wings puffed, flies off after it lowers its chest. I look at a tree in silence; a dog barks, another howls. The buds of the tree, all green, cannot keep me from the thought of walking along a riverbank to a tailor to fix my jacket. After the tailor, I imagine where I will go next – the park, or the market. When I awoke this morning, I did not feel like getting out of bed. The town cemetery is nearby. The tree is still in front of me, some branches waving in the chill, other leaves unmoving. Our neighbour has heaped bricks around the base of the trunk. What is exile but the inability to grow and flourish in the soil I have found myself in?

In the corner of a graveyard, a pile of clothes. Rooks sort through the array of shirts, dresses, socks, then move to the twigs on the earth. It has not rained; the ground is hard, cracking. If there was a sound to this, it would be the cry of a hen laying an egg. After, relieved, she would pick at seeds and dirt. The fence keeps her safe. An old headstone has faded; dandelions grow from its marble slab. What is inside can also be outside. Worms, for example, are normally found in soil, but not in the air. If they are seen, it is often during rain, or after, drying, desiccated; or when a rook pulls one out of the grass. I pull a thread on my jumper, ruin the seam. A pine tree breaks the pavement as it grows.

An apple tree is surrounded by bees. To be separated is to be unfulfilled. To not be in the unicity of the present. You will not find bees circling an ashen urn unless it is coated with pollen. At night, even though I am tired, I feel I can stay awake. Spring pulls out of winter, sometimes as a growing pain. And winter holds onto itself, releases only as it must, when the earth turns too far to one side. For years, refugees lie incarcerated in offshore detention centres. On the outskirts of town, one neighbour argues about the fence he shares. They take it to court, throw leftovers at dark, call each other names. This is not my town. I am just passing by.

Voice of America Shortwave Radio Towers Demolished
| JEN WEBB

This falling of towers against a backdrop of blue sky. How they turn toward each other, and fold, and fall, carrying from air to earth the memory of radio days when words conveyed ordinary stories to people living their wrapped-down lives, tuning the radio to their favourite station while they slice vegetables and steam rice and listen to news and sing along with the jingles as meanwhile their families make their random ways home. They have drifted off into history. The towers that sent the stories they lived by now fold up their limbs and depart the stage, changing from forms to glyphs. Threads of a story we can't read. Remnants of a time we can't recall.

Weather | ADAM AITKEN

While J. Clare the prophet, "by storms inspired,
Gazes in rapture on the troubled sky"
I don't think fading light in a battle scene
means what the defeated thought it meant,
(annihilation, slavery, pain)
or that rays of sunlight beamed down
on the Empire's fleet on the horizon
– each barque pregnant with spices –
was actually a sign of fortune,
ie, what Dutch masters thought it meant.
Maybe all this still applies.

Here, much fades like the curtains
in a French version of an Algerian boudoir,
curtains that were a bright lemon once
now some vulgar backdrop to a nude.

In the chateau, a decorator
made the rafters look "distressed"
and saved the owner thousands in tax.
So I won't invest in tarring the ship
as it lists in Flanders' evening glow.
Onshore the slaves mine the ground to dimness.
Tantalised they burn themselves like candles,
as thunderclouds backdrop the tower
at inflected angles.
Dark clouds of swifts arrive from Italy.
That is beautiful, rich in portent,
ominous cries from another republic.

when you get me alone | STU HATTON

after Sean Bonney (1969–2019)

when you get me alone,
take my biometrics
& your vengeance

& ask: do I live in fear
of gleaning too much
from the codes?

I fear those who await
the pre-ordained moment

while streets try to slip us
sketchy cartoons
of how flows're rigged:

a baggie of fentanyl
a rental squeeze
a kick in the cheek bone

because there are always other ways to lose

the apologists can cry amongst themselves
saying Sisyphus has never been happier

they know very well
on an undisclosed date
they can go & get fucked

(expletives are easy
in the dark)

but not everyone's flexing to survive

or squeezing whatever's left from the lime

not everything's a pill or sleepy melody
let alone friendly

whether speech or silence,
same denial

don't like our chances
when we forget how to move?

yeah, loneliness
yeah, a second-guessing loneliness
& a vicious sleep

what will absolve the kids
mining cobalt in the Congo
the maimed in Kyiv
the girl trafficked to a doorstep
she'll never cross again?

not some arrow of progress
shot at 45 degrees
from the mouth of the proxy—
snare-mouth of the body politic

find no comfort in the law
            in the riot
              in the haemorrhage
                      of the obvious

endings are hard, no joke

I've been holding back too long
(dusting a houseplant as it bleeds)

I'll speak my dust & be gone

Where it Lives | JINI MAXWELL

By the totem of a rabbit
In a week of ever softer landings

On a sheet doubling as a projector screen
As a flowerhorn swims into view

Through the light that crouches in the corner
While you are waking

In that first morning waking up next to you

In the part of me that once might have been polyester
That fills tentatively with organs again

In a diagram of a breast laid out like petals
Where I went looking for something more than gender, fate or
Meat that might be cancer

In an image of a future that doesn't make me afraid

Alongside two pumps of Testogel and another Christmas staying in the city
Between the brickwork, but not so deeply permeated yet

At a crossroads that is less of a choice and more of a marker
Here where I met you, where you were already walking

On this stretch of earth, in the smell of this gravel
Cinder blocks painted like candy out on a rented road

In the park after a movie while it was raining
In between two La Niñas, in preparation for a third

When you are close, when I hear my new voice saying
Just like that, that's it, right there

That's where it lives

willing | CLAIRE GASKIN

she was silver on wood   this lesion in blue tissue   worthwhile damage   I was really cold   the salt bush glitters on the tongue   today I resigned from servitude   the day the electricity company called saying my fuse box was sparking   releases the wax flower of solstice   happens where I land on the daunting   willing to clear   willing flame in glass   important event as a straight line with the earth   between the sun and strawberry wax flower moon tonight   thyme pink bells   the moonlight down the drive and side of the house   the flare in my legs   I am warm in this corner of couch

Without Poetry | LUKE FISCHER

In Memory of Adam Zagajewski

At times the bird taps its beak
on the window pane,
but at the wrong time, uninvited,
too much is pressing to be done.
I brush it away with my hand, but
as it flies off, glimpse the iridescent
turquoise feathers, sunset's embers.
The next afternoon the kingfisher
taps again. I'm doing my taxes—two years
overdue. Surely it should know to come
at a better time? In a whisper I explain
the matter to the bird, which tilts
its head with a thoughtful expression.
Uncomprehending, so it seems,
the kingfisher waits, perched on the sill.
I take out my calendar, circle April 4,
in two weeks' time. *Then would suit me well.*
And close the shutters. Dusk descends.
Night drapes a heavy cloth over everything
like the furniture and grand in a forgotten house.
Morning cannot lift the fabric, fine layers
of dust accumulate, each adding weight.
A week goes by, a month, two years.
Days roll on like a cargo train
sticking to its tracks.

Words with Bobby McGee | K A NELSON

Memories of you are buried in Baton Rouge.
These days I won't be one of the many exits
in the theatre of your marriage, so let's not
sacrifice truth for fantasy. Your separation
is a sham. You are far too cavalier with women's
hearts. If you were a real man, you'd confess
freedom means you want it all your way, in
Baton Rouge or New Orleans, but I leapt off
that diesel long ago. Your harmonica no longer
matches my song. I was right to call it, and glad
I didn't behave true to form and fall. Hesitation
was the right response to your exploration of
my world. I'm the Freedom Queen, a Janis J with
wings. I don't pester men for their time or money.
I'm no longer busted flat.

Two questions though—why do you keep booking
in to the same hotel as me? Do you want to keep
the fantasy central to your mind or mine?

Workarounds | DAN HOGAN

We completed tasks while your computer
was nonplussed. Never under any circumstances
outgather the USB cables as they are known
to the fossil record. Is anyone using this
rubric? A strongly worded mop bides here.
An epoch before us, an equivalent energy.
The moral to the story is a horny talkathon.
Posting generally is a captive curation. A scared

village buys now, pays later. Bags odourous
gains. Inside everywhere is time. Skeletons
made of other skeletons undergo workarounds.
Withdraw a like. Troubleshoot the jig if it starts
to look like your brain on internet, dollied blunt. Histories
of conspiratorial durdum are loading. Uh oh. A tiptoe
extravaganza engrooves serious laughlines. Deceives
blessedly. The droplets collecting on necks are owed

to the multipurpose fog. Order an adapter while
buff. Moths single out appliances to dent. Great
magistrates are coming your way. The depth
of a field is a streaming service. Who humours
the non-electric fence? Is it you who licks it clean?
Resemble the viral. Property the essential. Outdo
outcomes as opposed to going home on time. Plumb
the blameless. Countdown to glitches. Spondulix

when? Depolished chitchat, gutbucket sunrise. Lunch
on the old roof fizzles out. You can fail the creek.
But the bike. The bike is in the creek. Bestow
little quizzes. Then the second moment of area (clue:
see toward a federation of etcetera crises). Surface

a length of singsong worseness, refranchise exquisite
doldrums. Swanky exits expect better. It is time for
your next marathonic ache. Enrapture well, dear salad

and lots of mozzies. An existential kneecapping.
Real windsock hours. Unhallowed visits from
tricky miniatures clog the month. Eventually,
prescriptions. Entablature. Maximum research.
Netlike greenth. Bigheadedly nod if you want
to defragment. Reevaluate persuasions over mild
interludes. Up the revelry. Roster on fleetingness.
Consult moments. Misallocate enthusiasm for

stakeholders. Dream-eating surucucus warm the
pit. Indispensable attunements are down the hall.
Minimalism is for jerk apologists. According to
resorts the cement world is everything a unit of
productivity could want. Put it this way: the forest
wasn't November. Allegedly joyless. Heart an
an infographic. Repot survival news. Favourite
an unopened secret.

Wrong Forest | MICHAEL FARRELL

Seven candles in flame trembled; birds chirped in excelsis;
whistling 'Trouble'. To what extent I could blame the forest,
I couldn't say. Affirming shadows, widows, indolent sons,
for five trade depots, hastening, itching. I had destroyed
the family fortune, so I went seeking another. My cherub,
assiduous, tolerant, damning few mistakes, sweetly ignorant,
miming 'Pamela'. Punishing myself, I sold my favourite
daughter to a cotton mill. The rest read novels all day: I couldn't
expect any help there. That havoc ailed everyone, consoled
indeed, debts accumulated, no rent ready, taxes. Beware Flaubert.
   Choose Balzac? No Diderot, or Racine, provided nuts,
Armagnac. A new program result: Oasis deserved 0.05% blame /
credit for Brexit. Travelling. Faded hopes by dinner. Keeping my
wits for the interruption. In the forest were many knights'
decaying bodies hanging from trees. I'd resolved to press on; or
my horse refused to reverse. Rubbing the rifle. Hurrying,
making offers, orisons, penance, though really imaginary. Past
a castle, burnt hedges, no animals, charcoal everywhere,
whistling 'Teardrops'. To what extent can a national history
be considered a play? Eerily elated, hamstrung, anxious, the time
melted through wood, rushed on. One route would've taken me
to Titania, and her enslaved elves. Every bell and violin, organ
peal, played tunes that intimated benison. But I'd taken
the predestined path of violence, and bloody endurance. Guess
away, jury, whether days, tomorrows mattered, after honourably
braving it. I believed hacking a murderer to death was just
and glorious.

You draw the heart | BETH SPENCER

after 'Portrait' by Louise Glück

Can it fit this cage of body?
Those ribs, hungry.

Cat paws at it.
The beat is a song.

Why go there? Why leave
that trail of meat ribbons?

Gather brush. Sweep up
mess, blood tears.

Stuff it back down into bone
cave. Add flesh to silence.

The cat yawns. We have
done this so many times.

Aren't you tired of it yet?

You Speak Clouds | ANDY JACKSON

Asked how you are, you speak clouds. Or erasures. In the pages of your diary, flakes of ash, a drift of full stops. Your blackened hands fidget. Asked your name, you turn to the window, thinking of elsewhere. The absurd, handsome face of the Christmas Island Frigatebird. The keen yellow eyes of the Western Swamp Tortoise. Such losses, beyond you and close. It's like they say; makes it harder, the more you love. Your hair in the sink. Nights awake, listening. Body adrift. Asked what's on your mind, you open your arms, as if to say, *this, all of this*.

After the digital drawing collage of the same name by Rachael Wenona Guy (2024). The phrase "makes it harder, the more you love" is from the song "The Watershed" by Mark Hollis.

CONTRIBUTORS
& ACKNOWLEDGEMENTS

Notes on Contributors

Adam Aitken lives in Sydney and France. His last book was *Revenants* (Giramondo). He received the Patrick White Award in 2022.

Chris Andrews' third collection of poems is *The Oblong Plot* (Puncher & Wattmann, 2024). His study of the Oulipo, *How to Do Things with Forms*, was published by McGill-Queen's University Press in 2022. He has translated books of prose fiction, including Ágota Kristóf's *I Don't Care* (New Directions, 2024), Liliana Colanzi's *You Glow in the Dark* (New Directions, 2024), and César Aira's *The Lime Tree* (And Other Stories, 2017).

Manisha Anjali is the author of *Naag Mountain* (Giramondo, 2024). She is the founder of *Neptune*, a research and documentation platform for dreams, visions and hallucinations. She has lived in Fiji, Aotearoa and Australia.

Stuart Barnes is the author of *Like to the Lark* (Upswell Publishing), winner of the 2023 Wesley Michel Wright Prize in Poetry, shortlisted for the 2024 ALS Gold Medal and highly commended in the 2024 NSW Premier's Literary Awards, and of *Glasshouses* (UQP), winner of the 2015 Arts Queensland Thomas Shapcott Poetry Prize, commended in the 2016 Anne Elder Award and shortlisted for the 2017 Mary Gilmore Award. Stuart, Nigel Featherstone, Melinda Smith and CJ Bowerbird are Hell Herons, a spokenword+music collective whose first record *The Wreck Event* is out now at Bandcamp and on all major streaming platforms.

Ender Başkan lives and works in Narrm/Melbourne, Australia. He is a poet, bookseller and co-founder of Vre Books press. His novel *A Portrait of Alice as a Young Man* was published in 2019. He is the winner of the 2021 *Overland* Judith Wright Poetry Prize.

Damien Becker is a disabled writer and performer from Murwillumbah, NSW. An award-winning spoken word artist known for exploring the relationship of disability and terminal illness to memory and the social self, his poetry has been published by *Australian Poetry Journal*, *Verity La*, *Bramble Journal*, *Sunder Journal*, and *Regional Review*, among others. He lives with cystic fibrosis and had a double-lung transplant in 2015.

Judith Beveridge has published eight books of poetry, mostly recently *Tintinnabulum* (Giramondo Publishing, 2024). She was poetry editor of *Meanjin* for 10 years and taught poetry writing for 16 years at post-graduate level at the University of Sydney. Her books have won major prizes including the 2019 Prime Minister's Award for Poetry for *Sun Music: New and Selected Poems*. She lives in Sydney.

A selection of **Ken Bolton**'s collaborative writing with John Jenkins, *A Double Act*, appeared in 2023 from Puncher & Wattmann. His more recent books include *Threefer* and *Salute* (Puncher & Wattmann), *Starting at Basheer's* and *London Journal* both from Vagabond Press; and *Lonnie's Lament* from Wakefield Press, which, beginning in 2019, issued the collaborations with Peter Bakowski—*Elsewhere Variations*, *Nearly Lunch*, *Waldo's Game* and *On Luck Street* (2023). Bolton's recent collections *Fantastic Day* (2022) and *Metropole* (2024) appeared from Puncher & Wattmann. *Cordite* published *A Pirate Life* in 2023.

Pam Brown has been writing, collaborating, editing & publishing in diverse modes both locally & internationally for decades. Some of her books have been on the shortlists and have sometimes won the prize. Pam's most recent collection of poems is *Stasis Shuffle* (Hunter Publishers, 2021).

Melinda Bufton is the author of collections *Girlery* and *Superette*. In 2019, she was the winner of the Charles Rischbieth Jury Poetry Prize as well as the Helen Anne Bell Poetry Bequest Award, the latter resulting in the publication of her third collection, *Moxie*.

joanne burns is a Sydney poet.

Pascalle Burton is a Meanjin-based experimental poet and performer with an interest in conceptual art and cultural theory. She also plays in the band The Stress of Leisure. Her collection *About the Author is Dead* is available through Cordite Books and the collaborative project *Author Unknown* (with David Stavanger) is online at Red Room Poetry.

aj carruthers is the 2024 recipient of the Cy Twombly Award for Poetry, from the Foundation for Contemporary Arts (FCA). Books include *Languages of Invention: Literary History and Avant-Garde Poetics in the Antipodes* (Edinburgh University Press, 2024), the first study of Australian avant-garde poetry, three volumes of the lifelong long poem *AXIS*, being *AXIS Z Book 3* (Cordite, 2023), *AXIS Book 2* (Vagabond, 2019), and *AXIS Book 1: 'Areal'* (Vagabond, 2014), and *Stave Sightings: Notational Experiments in North American Long Poems, 1961–2011* (Palgrave, 2017). Additionally he has composed and performed the *Consonata*, a half-hour long Sound Poem, and writes occasional journalism on local and international affairs. He lived and worked in China for half a decade, as Associate Professor at Nanjing University, Lecturer at Shanghai University of International Business and Economics (S.U.I.B.E.), and is currently a Visiting Fellow at the Australian National University.

Luoyang Chen is the author of *Flow* (Red River/Centre for Stories, 2023).

Eileen Chong is a poet of Hakka, Hokkien and Peranakan descent. She is the author of nine books. *We Speak of Flowers* is forthcoming with UQP in 2025. She lives and works on unceded Gadigal land of the Eora Nation.

Aidan Coleman has published three collections of poetry, most recently *Mount Sumptuous* (Wakefield, 2020). He teaches Creative Writing and English Education at Southern Cross University on the Gold Coast.

Emilie Collyer lives on unceded Wurundjeri Country in Australia where she writes across forms. Her poetry book *Do you have anything less domestic?* (Vagabond Press 2022) won the inaugural Five Islands Press Prize. Emilie recently completed a PhD researching feminist practice at RMIT, where she is now an Adjunct Industry Fellow.

Stuart Cooke is a poet, essayist and translator. His fourth collection of poems, *The grass is greener over your grave*, was published by Puncher & Wattmann in 2023.

Ion Corcos was born in Sydney, Australia in 1969. He has been published in *Cordite, Meanjin, Westerly, Plumwood Mountain, Southword, Wild Court, riddlebird*, and other journals. Ion is a nature lover and a supporter of animal rights. He is the author of *A Spoon of Honey* (Flutter Press, 2018).

Kathryn Crowcroft's writing has appeared in *Prototype, HEAT* literary journal, *Lit Hub, The Best Australian Poems* series, *Weekend Review* national newspaper magazine and the *Australian Poetry Journal* multiple times, *Visual Verse*, and other media. She completed her doctorate at the University of Cambridge where she won the John Kinsella and Brewer Hall prizes for poetry.

Amy Crutchfield is a poet. Her work has been published in Australia, the UK and Ireland. Her first collection *The Cyprian* (Giramondo) was published in 2023 and received the Prime Minister's Literary Award in 2024.

Nathan Curnow is a multi-award winning poet, playwright, spoken word performer and author of six collections, including *The Ghost Poetry Project* and *The Apocalypse Awards*. He has taught creative writing at Federation University, judged numerous prizes and toured Europe in 2018 with Geoffrey Williams, opening the Heidelberg Literary Days Festival in Germany. His latest collection, *A Hill to Die On*, is published by Liquid Amber Press.

Gabriel Curtin is an artist, writer and editor living as an uninvited guest on unceded Gadigal Country. His work broadly considers poetry's ability to locate and enact relations unencumbered by policy.

Tricia Dearborn is an award-winning Australian poet, writer and editor. She has had three full-length collections and a chapbook published. Her latest collection is *Autobiochemistry* (UWAP, 2019). Composer Elliott Gyger's 'Autobiochemistry', based on thirteen poems from that book, won the 2022 Paul Lowin Song Cycle Prize. Tricia has judged poetry competitions, including the 2019 University of Canberra VC's International Poetry Prize, and been guest poetry editor for various literary journals, most recently for *Cordite Poetry Review 112: TREAT* (May 2024).

Benjamin Dodds grew up in the NSW Riverina and studied at the University of Sydney. He is the author of *Regulator* (Puncher & Wattmann, 2014) and *Airplane Baby Banana Blanket* (Recent Work Press, 2020), which was shortlisted for the Judith Wright Calanthe Award and the international Poetry Book Award. He has served as a judge for the Quantum Words Science Poetry Competition and the Val Vallis Award and as a reader for Overland. His next collection, *The Ease of Eggs*, is forthcoming from Five Islands Press in 2025.

Australian **Cath Drake** is based in London. She was an award-winning environmental journalist and writer in Australia for a decade. Her poetry collection, *The Shaking City* (Seren Books), longlisted in the international Laurel Prize, highly commended in the UK Forward Prize, followed *Sleeping with Rivers*, Poetry Book Society choice and winner of the Seren/Mslexia pamphlet prize. Other prizes include twice second place in the *Ginkgo* eco-poetry prize. She has been published widely in anthologies and literary journals internationally. Cath is also a mindfulness teacher and she hosts *The Verandah*, quality online poetry events.

Dave Drayton was an amateur banjo player, founding member of the Atterton Academy, and the author of *British P(oe)Ms* (Beir Bua Press), *E, UIO, A* (Container), *P(oe)Ms* (Rabbit), *Haiturograms* (SOd Press) and other works.

Willo Drummond's debut poetry collection *Moon Wrasse* (Puncher & Wattmann), was shortlisted for the Kenneth Slessor Prize for Poetry in the 2024 NSW Premier's Literary Awards, commended in the 2023 Five Islands Poetry Prize for a First Book of Poetry and selected as one of 6 Australian poetry titles to feature in the 2024 Aesop Queer Library. Willo's poetry has been shortlisted for the Val Vallis Award, the South Coast Writers Centre Poetry Award and runner-up in the Tom Collins Poetry Prize. In 2023–24 she co-edited, with poet Stuart Barnes, 'Queering Ecopoet(h)ics', a queer themed issue of *Plumwood Mountain Journal*.

Michelle D'Souza (aka Michelle Cahill, pronouns she/they) is an Indian Australian poet, whose published collections are *Vishvarupa*, *The Accidental Cage*, *Night Birds*, and *The Herring Lass*. Her awards include the Val Vallis Award, the Red Room Poetry Fellowship, the Helen Ann Bell Bequest shortlist, the Newcastle Poetry Prize shortlist, and the ABR Peter Porter Prize shortlist. Cordite Poetry are publishing a new collection, titled, *Blaze*.

Laurie Duggan was involved in the poetry worlds of Melbourne and Sydney through the 1970s and 80s. He lived in England from 2006 until 2018 when he returned to Sydney. His most recent books are *A kite hangs above the border* (Macau, Flying Islands, 2022), *Homer Street* (Giramondo 2020) and *Selected Poems 1971–2017* (Shearsman 2018). *The New Weather* is forthcoming in 2025.

Michael Farrell is from Bombala, NSW, and has lived in Melbourne since 1990. Recent book publications are *Googlecholia* (Giramondo 2022) and *Family Trees* (Giramondo 2020). Michael has written chapters on colonial poetry, for both the *Cambridge Companion to Australian Poetry* (2024), and the *Cambridge History of Australian Poetry* (2025).

Liam Ferney's most recent collection, *Hot Take* (Hunter Publishing), was shortlisted for the Judith Wright Calanthe Award. His other collections include *Content* (Hunter Publishing) and *Boom* (Grande Parade Poets). He lives in Brisbane, Australia with his wife and daughter. He works in public affairs in the health sector.

Luke Fischer is a poet and philosopher. His books include the poetry collections *A Gamble for my Daughter* (Vagabond Press, 2022), *A Personal History of Vision* (UWAP, 2017) and *Paths of Flight* (Black Pepper, 2013), the monograph *The Poet as Phenomenologist: Rilke and the 'New Poems'* (Bloomsbury, 2015) and the philosophical work *Philosophical Fragments as the Poetry of Thinking* (Bloomsbury, 2024). Fischer holds a PhD from the University of Sydney where he is also an honorary associate in philosophy.

Toby Fitch (he/they) is poetry editor of *Overland* and a lecturer in creative writing at the University of Sydney, on Gadigal land. Author of eight books of poetry, including *Where Only the Sky had Hung Before* (2019), *Sydney Spleen* (2021) and *Object Permanence: Calligrammes* (2022), he is currently writing a book called *Endlings*.

Jo Gardiner lives on Gundungurra country in the Blue Mountains. She has been a finalist in the Montreal International Poetry Prize, The Newcastle Poetry Prize, the ACU Poetry prize and the University of Canberra Vice Chancellor's International Poetry Prize. Her work has appeared in *Island*, *Meanjin* and *Westerly*. Her novel, *The Concerto Inn*, was published by UWA Publishing in 2006. She holds a PhD in Communication and Media from Western Sydney University. Her debut poetry collection, *The Impossible Shore*, is published by Vagabond Press (2024).

Angela Gardner, writer and visual artist, has six poetry collections. *Slippage*, her manuscript-in-progress, was shortlisted for the Helen Anne Bell Poetry Bequest Award 2023. Her verse novel *The Sorry Tale of the Mignonette*, was shortlisted for Wales Book of the Year, 2022 and a UK National Poetry Day recommendation.

Claire Gaskin completed her first full-length poetry collection *a bud* assisted by an Australia Council grant (now Creative Australia). *A bud* was released by John Leonard Press in 2006 and was shortlisted in the John Bray SA Festival Awards for Literature. *Paperweight* was published in 2013 by Hunter Publishers. *Eurydice Speaks* was published by Hunter Publishers in 2021. *Ismene's Survivable Resistance* was completed as the creative component of her PhD in Writing and Literature at Deakin University and was published by Puncher & Wattmann in 2021. Her next full length poetry collection is being written assisted by Creative Australia.

Jake Goetz has published three collections of poetry: *meditations with passing water* (Rabbit Poets Series, 2018), which was shortlisted for the Queensland Premier's Award; *Unplanned Encounters: Poems 2015–2020* (Apothecary Archive, 2023); and most recently, *Holocene Pointbreaks* (Puncher & Wattmann, 2024).

Rory Green is a writer, editor and digital media artist living on Awabakal country in Australia. They are co-editor of digital literary journal Crawlspace and are publishing a poem for every Pokémon through the newsletter project Otherwise Pokedex.

Kerry Greer is an Irish-Australian poet and writer. She received the Venie Holmgren Prize for Environmental Poetry in 2021. Kerry has been shortlisted for the Elizabeth Jolley Short Story Prize, the Calibre Essay Prize, the Woollahra Digital Literary Award, the Newcastle Poetry Prize, the ACU Poetry Prize, the Gwen Harwood Poetry Prize, and more. She holds an MFA in Poetry from Cedar Crest College. Her debut poetry collection, *The Sea Chest*, was published by Recent Work Press in 2023.

Madison Griffiths is an author, artist and producer. Her debut book *Tissue* (Ultimo Press) was released in 2023, and is a boldly poetic meditation on abortion and what it has the power to represent. She is the co-producer of *Tender*, a podcast that tracks the journey of individuals as they decide to leave an abusive relationship. In 2022, she was awarded the Walkley Foundation Our Watch Award for Excellence in Reporting on Violence Against Women, alongside co-producer, Beth Atkinson-Quinton. Her work largely centres around the lived experiences of women, especially those whose realities are shrouded in stigma, opposition and rebellion.

Stu Hatton is a writer/editor who lives on unceded Djaara country near Castlemaine, Victoria. His work has featured in *The Age*, *Australian Poetry Journal*, *Best Australian Poems 2012*, *Cordite*, *Overland*, *Rabbit*, *Southerly*, and *Westerly*. Stu's third poetry collection, *In the Not-too-distant Present*, will be published in 2024 by Outer Publishing.

Ashley Haywood is an award-winning writer whose work often moves in the art-science nexus. She is the author of *Polyp* (Vagabond Press, 2024). She lives on Kabi Kabi and Ningy Ningy Lands.

Dan Hogan (they/them) is the author of *Secret Third Thing*, which won the Mary Gilmore Award and the Five Islands Prize, and was named one of the 'best 25 Australian books of 2023' by *The Guardian*. Dan's poetry has been recognised by the Peter Porter Poetry Prize, Judith Wright Poetry Prize, and Val Vallis Award, among others. Dan runs DIY publisher Subbed In and edits the working-class literary journal *Industrial Estate*.

LK Holt has published six books; her most recent is *Three Books* (2024). Her books have won the Queensland Literary Award for Poetry (the Judith Wright Calanthe Award), the New South Wales Premier's Award for Poetry (the Kenneth Slessor Prize), and the Grace Leven Prize. Her books have been shortlisted for the Prime Minister's Award for Poetry and the Victorian Premier's Award for Poetry, and longlisted for the Australian Literature Society's Gold Medal. She lives in Narrm/Melbourne.

Duncan Bruce Hose is a poet, visual artist and essayist. His published books include *The Lumpen Aristocrats* (now orries press 2024), *Testacles Gone Walkabout* (Slow Loris 2021), *The Jewelled Shillelagh* (Puncher and Wattman 2019), *Bunratty* (Puncher 2015), *A Book of Sea-Shanty* (Bulky News Press 2014), *One Under Bacchus* (Inken Publisch 2011) and *Rathaus* (Inken 2007). His first critical monograph, entitled *The Pursuit of Myth in the Poetry of Frank O'Hara, Ted Berrigan and John Forbes: Prick'd by Charm* (Modern and Contemporary Poetry and Poetics), was published by Palgrave Macmillan in 2022.

Lulu Houdini is a Gamilaroi poet and midwife. Lulu's work explores invisibility, memory, resistance, and liminality.

Davoren Howard is a Victorian writer, living on unceded Boon Wurrung land. He has been longlisted for the Montreal and Bridport PP's, shortlisted for the Blake and Bridport PP's, and published in *Cordite Poetry Review* and *Australian Poetry Anthology*.

Andy Jackson is a disabled poet, essayist, creative writing teacher at the University of Melbourne, and a Patron of Writers Victoria. His latest poetry collection is *Human Looking*, which won the ALS Gold Medal and the Prime Minister's Literary Award for Poetry. He writes and rests on Dja Dja Wurrung country.

Anna Jacobson is an award-winning writer, artist, and researcher from Meanjin (Brisbane). Her memoir *How to Knit a Human* was published with NewSouth in 2024. *Amnesia Findings* (UQP, 2019) won the Thomas Shapcott Poetry Prize. Her second poetry collection *Anxious in a Sweet Store* (Upswell, 2023) won an Australian Jewish Book Award. *All Rage Blaze Light*, Anna's third poetry collection, is forthcoming with Upswell in 2025. She received a 2023 Outstanding Doctoral Thesis Award from Queensland University of Technology.

Hannah Jenkins is an arts writer and poet specialising in digital platforms and online writing experiments. Their work frequently considers imagined landscapes and the poetic composability of data. Hannah is the co-founder of *Crawlspace.cool* and was previously Assistant Editor and Poetry Editor of *Running Dog*. You can find Hannah's work in *Cordite*, *Overland*, *Taper*, *The HTML Review* and much more.

Jill Jones lives on unceded Kaurna land. Her latest book is *Acrobat Music: New & Selected Poems*, longlisted for the 2024 ALS Gold Medal. Other recent books include *Wild Curious Air*, winner of the 2021 Wesley Michel Wright Prize, and *A History Of What I'll Become*, shortlisted for the 2021 Kenneth Slessor Award and the 2022 John Bray Award. In 2015 she won the Victorian Premier's Prize for Poetry for *The Beautiful Anxiety*. Her work is widely published in Australia, Canada, Ireland, NZ, Singapore, Sweden, UK, and USA.

Georgia/George Kartas is a writer, researcher and performer living in Naarm. George co-runs quarterly poetry event *Thin Red Lines*, and is a bookseller, tarot reader, and the Reviews Editor of *KalliopeX*. Created as part of the 2020 Wheeler Centre Hot Desk Fellowship, their collaborative poetry-sound album with Lucas George, *Mythamorphosis*, is out now.

Cath Kenneally is a poet, novelist, broadcaster and arts journalist. Her *Around Here* won the John Bray Poetry Award. Her latest manuscript is *The Green Room*, her eighth book of poems.

Louis Klee is an Australian writer and philosopher. He teaches at the University of Cambridge, where he is a fellow and assistant professor at Trinity Hall. A draft of his novel *Qualms* was a finalist for the 2023 Deborah Rogers Foundation Writers Award, which was judged by a panel chaired by Abdulrazak Gurnah. He has contributed to the *Sydney Review of Books* as a JUNCTURE Fellow, which presents 'a series of new essays… by leading critics'. In 2023, he was writer-in-residence at the Centre for Australian Literary Cultures.

Jaye Kranz is a writer and documentary audio maker living in Naarm/Melbourne on the unceded lands of the Wurundjeri Woi Wurrung People. She is the recipient of an Emerging Writers Grant from the Australia Council for the Arts (now Creative Australia). Her work has appeared in *The Monthly*, *Australian Book Review*, short story collections and a compendium of four novellas (Picador, Vintage), with poems forthcoming in *West Branch* and *The Florida Review*. She was shortlisted for the Tom Collins Poetry Prize. Her sound-rich audio features have been commissioned for BBC Radio 4, BBC Radio 3, ABC RN, and Arts Centre Melbourne.

Jeanine Leane is an activist, poet, writer and teacher who belongs to the Wiradjuri people of the Murrumbidgee River near Gundagai. Jeanine currently lives and work on the lands of the East Kulin Nations of Naarm, Melbourne.

Harold Legaspi is an Australian writer born in Manila, Philippines, and living in unceded Darug Nura (Western Sydney, Australia). Harold's books include *Letters in Language* (Flying Islands) and *Bahay Kubo: Children's Literature* (Papel Publishing). He holds a Doctor of Arts from University of Sydney. Harold was the English-as-Second-Language winner in The 2023 Best Australian Yarn. Other poetry collections include *Litany*, *Requiem* and *Edge of Seas vs Lost Generation* (University of Sydney).

Debbie Lim received the 2022 Bruce Dawe National Poetry Prize. She was shortlisted for the 2022 Peter Porter Poetry Prize. Her chapbook is *Beastly Eye* (Vagabond Press) and a full-length collection will be published by Cordite Books in 2025. She was born in Sydney, where she lives on Darramuragal land.

Janaka Malwatta was born in Sri Lanka, grew up in London, and now spends his time between Sri Lanka and Brisbane. He won the 2021 Arts Queensland Thomas Shapcott Poetry Prize for *blackbirds don't mate with starlings*, which was published by University of Queensland Press in 2022. He has appeared at Brisbane Writers Festival, the OzAsia Festival and at Queensland Poetry Festival. He has been published in various magazines, including *Cordite Poetry Review*, *Rabbit Poetry Journal* and *Peril Magazine*.

Julie Manning is a poet and artist. Her poetry has been shortlisted in the Peter Porter Poetry prize, Blake Poetry prize, Newcastle Poetry prize and Aesthetica Creative Writing Award (UK) and appeared in *ABR*, *Meanjin*, *Overland* and other publications and anthologies. She lives in bayside Brisbane.

Shey Marque is a former medical and research scientist. Her most recent poetry collection, *The Hum Hearers* (UWAP 2025) was shortlisted for the Dorothy Hewett Award 2023. *Keeper of the Ritual* (UWAP 2019) was shortlisted for the Noel Rowe Award. She currently coordinates the Hospital Poets Program WA, and serves as Board Secretary of Writing WA.

Jini Maxwell is a poet and curator based in Naarm. They curate videogames for work, and write trans poems for their friends.

Chloe Mayne is descended from the trawlwoolway people of lutruwita's northeast. Her work moves in the realms of mothering, decoloniality and ecology. She is writing a creative doctorate at the University of the Sunshine Coast, and is a current recipient of the Marten Bequest for Poetry.

Scott-Patrick Mitchell was the recipient of the 2022 Red Room Poetry Fellowship, the 2023 XYZ Prize for Innovation in Spoken Word and was Highly Commended in the 2024 Blake Poetry Prize. Their debut poetry collection *Clean* (Upswell Publishing, 2022) was shortlisted for The Prime Minister's Literary Awards, The WA Premier's Book Awards and The Victorian Premier's Literary Awards.

K A Nelson won the *Overland* Judith Wright Poetry Prize for New and Emerging Poets in 2010. Since then she has published individual poems in many Australian publications and anthologies. She has two collections: *Inlandia* (2018) and *Meaty Bones* (2023) both published by Recent Work Press, both highly commended in the ACT Writers' Centre publishing awards. She also received a Canberra Critics Circle Award for *Meaty Bones*, in 2023.

Damen O'Brien is a multi-award-winning poet based in Brisbane. Damen's prizes include The Moth Poetry Prize and the Peter Porter Poetry Prize. His poems have been published in *Arc Poetry Magazine*, *New Ohio Review*, *Poetry Wales* and other journals. Damen's latest book is *Walking the Boundary*, published by Pitt Street Poetry.

Roslyn Orlando is an artist, writer and gardener based in Melbourne on Wurundjeri Country. Her writing and artistic works explore relationships between language, history and technology. She studied journalism at the University of Sydney, and Arts Politics at Tisch School of the Arts, New York University.

Esther Ottaway is a Tasmanian/lutruwita poet, editor and mentor who has won or been shortlisted for global prizes including the Tom Collins, Woorilla, MPU International, Mslexia, Bridport, Montreal, and Tim Thorne Prize for Poetry. Her acclaimed new collection, *She Doesn't Seem Autistic*, poetically lifts the lid on bright girls with hidden autism, who are going undiagnosed and unsupported in a medical system designed for boys. In 2024, Esther will release a landmark anthology of disability writing, co-edited with Andy Jackson and Kerri Shying, titled *Raging Grace: Australian writers speak out on disability* (Puncher & Wattmann).

Felicity Plunkett is a poet and critic living on Wangal land. Her books are *A Kinder Sea* (UQP), *Vanishing Point* (UQP) and *Seastrands* (Vagabond). She edited *Thirty Australian Poets* (UQP). Felicity has a PhD from the University of Sydney and was Poetry Editor with University of Queensland Press for nine years.

Claire Potter is author of two collections, *Swallow* (Five Islands Press 2010) and *Acanthus* (Giramondo 2022).

Stephanie Powell is a poet based in Naarm / Melbourne. Her forthcoming collection is *Invisible Wasp* (Liquid Amber Press, 2024). *Gentle Creatures* was published by Vagabond Press in 2023. Her work has been translated into Spanish, Braille and published widely. atticpoet.com

David Prater is an Australian-born writer currently living in the Netherlands. His works include *We Will Disappear* (papertiger media, 2007), *Morgenland* (Vagabond Press, 2007) and *Leaves of Glass* (Puncher and Wattmann, 2014). Between 2001 and 2012, he was Managing Editor of *Cordite Poetry Review*.

Nadia Rhook is a white settler historian, poet, and educator, living and writing on unceded Wurundjeri-Woi Worrung Country. Nadia is the author of two history-themed poetry collections: *boots* (UWA Publishing, 2020) and *Second Fleet Baby* (Fremantle Press, 2022). Her writing also appears in such scholarly and creative places as the *Journal of Postcolonial Studies*, *Westerly*, *Cordite*, and is anthologised in Australian Poetry's *Best of Australian Poems 2022* and *What We Carry: Poetry on Childbearing* (Recent Work Press, 2022). She can currently be found writing awe-struck poems about stone.

Claire Miranda Roberts is a poet and professional copy editor based in Melbourne. Her poetry has been shortlisted and commended in several international literary competitions, including the Oxford Brookes International Poetry Prize 2020 and the Stephen Spender Prize 2021. The working manuscript for her first collection *Kangaroo Paw* (Vagabond Press 2023) was shortlisted for the 2021 Helen Anne Bell Poetry Bequest Award – Australia's richest poetry prize for women. Most recently, *Kangaroo Paw* was shortlisted for the Victorian Premier's Literary Award for poetry.

Autumn Royal creates drama, poetry and criticism on unceded Wurundjeri Woi Wurrung land. Autumn is an arts worker, sessional academic and Interviews Editor at *Cordite Poetry Review*. Her poetry collections include *She Woke and Rose*, *Liquidation* and *The Drama Student*, which was shortlisted for the 2023 Queensland Premier's Judith Wright Calanthe Award and the 2024 Prime Minister's Literary Award for Poetry.

Gig Ryan's *New and Selected Poems* (Giramondo, 2011); *Selected Poems* (Bloodaxe, 2012), was winner of the 2012 Grace Leven Prize for Poetry and the 2012 Kenneth Slessor Prize for Poetry. She has also written songs with Disband, Six Goodbyes (1988), Driving Past, Real Estate (1999) and Travel (2006). She was Poetry Editor of *The Age* 1998–2016, and is a regular poetry reviewer, and is continuing work on her next book of poems.

Sara M Saleh is a writer/poet, human rights lawyer, and the daughter of Palestinian, Lebanese and Egyptian migrants. Her poems, essays and short stories have been published widely and she is co-editor of the ground-breaking 2019 anthology *Arab, Australian, Other: Stories on Race and Identity*. Her first novel is *Songs for the Dead and the Living* (Affirm Press, 2023), which was shortlisted for the 2024 NSW Premier's Awards. Her first poetry collection is *The Flirtation of Girls/ Ghazal el-Banat* (UQP, 2023), which was shortlisted for the 2024 ALS Gold Medal and won the Anne Elder Award. Sara is the first poet to win both the 2021 Peter Porter Poetry Prize and the 2020 Judith Wright Poetry Prize. She is the recipient of the inaugural Affirm fellowship for Sweatshop writers, a Neilma Sidney travel grant, Varuna writers residency, and Amant writers residency in Brooklyn, New York, amongst other honours. Sara is based on Bidjigal land with her partner and their beloved three cats and pup.

Omar Sakr is a writer who opposes the genocide of Palestine, and racist imperialist violences everywhere. He is the son of Arab and Turkish Muslim migrants, and the author of three poetry collections, most recently *Non-Essential Work* (UQP, 2023), as well as a novel, *Son of Sin* (the87press, 2024). He lives on unceded Dharug land.

Ella Skilbeck-Porter is a poet based in Melbourne/Naarm on unceded Wurundjeri Country. Her debut collection of poetry and visual poetry *These Are Different Waters* (Vagabond 2023) was highly commended in the Anne Elder Award and shortlisted for the Helen Anne Bell Poetry Bequest and the Mary Gilmore Award.

Ali Jane Smith's poetry has been published in literary journals and her collection *Strange Matter* is forthcoming from Life Before Man books. She lives in Wollongong, on the land of the Wodi Wodi Dharawhal people.

Barnaby Smith is a poet, critic, journalist and musician living on Darug and Gundungurra / the Blue Mountains. Recent work has appeared in journals such as *Stand, Blackbox Manifold, 3AM, Erbacce, Orbis, Tentacular, Molly Bloom* and *Blaze Vox,* as well as *Cordite, Southerly, Australian Poetry Journal, Australian Poetry Anthology, Best Australian Poems,* and more. He is an award-winning art and music critic, and records music under the name Brigadoon, having released the album, *Itch Factor,* in 2020.

Hazel Smith is a poet, performer, electronic writer and scholar. Her five volumes of poetry include *Word Migrants,* Giramondo, 2016, *Ecliptical,* ES-Press, Spineless Wonders, 2022 and *Heimlich Unheimlich* — with Sieglinde Karl-Spence — Apothecary Archive, 2024. She has published numerous performance and multimedia works and is a founding member of the multimedia ensemble austraLYSIS. In 2018, with Will Luers and Roger Dean, she won the Electronic Literature Organisation's Robert Coover prize. Hazel is an Emeritus Professor in the Writing and Society Research Centre, Western Sydney University. She has authored several academic books including *The Contemporary Literature-Music Relationship,* Routledge, 2016.

Beth Spencer writes across the boundaries of poetry, memoir, fiction and essay. Her books include *The Age of Fibs*, *Vagabondage* and *The Party of Life*. She lives and writes on unceded Darkinjung land.

David Stavanger is a poet, producer, parent, and lapsed psychologist living on Dharawal land. He is the co-editor of *Admissions: Voices Within Mental Health* (Upswell, 2022). David's last collection *Case Notes* (UWAP, 2020) won the 2021 Victorian Premier's Literary Award for Poetry, and his next collection, *The Drop Off*, is forthcoming with Upswell Publishing in 2025.

Thom Sullivan is a writer, editor and reviewer of poetry. His debut book of poems, *Carte Blanche* (Vagabond Press, 2019), won the Noel Rowe Poetry Award and the 2020 Mary Gilmore Award. He grew up in Wistow/Bugle Ranges in the Mount Lofty Ranges, South Australia, and now lives in Adelaide, where he works in public policy.

Josie/Jocelyn Suzanne is a freelance editor/writer/programmer. Her work has appeared in *Cordite*, *Southerly*, *Rabbit Journal* and *Overland*, among others. She was shortlisted for the Val Vallis award in 2022, was the winner of the 2021 Harri Jones memorial prize and was one of the 2021 Next Chapter recipients. She is a genderqueer trans femme, living on unceded Wurundjeri land in Naarm.

Munira Tabassum Ahmed is a 19-year-old writer. Her work has been published in *Frontier*, *Meanjin*, *Liminal*, *Red Room Poetry*, *Cordite*, and elsewhere. She was the 2022 Kat Muscat Fellow, 2024 WestWords Accelerator Recipient, and is currently working on her first novel.

Thabani Tshuma is a multi-award-winning Zimbabwean writer and performance poet. His work can be found in publications such as *Dichotomi* magazine, *Cordite Poetry Review*, *CUBBY ART*, and ABC ArtWorks' *SLAMMED* segment. Thabani is co-curator of *Thin Red Lines* and his debut collection, *The Gospel of Unmade Creation*, was released in 2023 through Recent Work Press.

Ann Vickery is the author of *Bees Do Bother: An Antagonist's Care Pack* (Vagabond Press, 2021), *Devious Intimacy* (Hunter Publishers, 2015), and *The Complete Pocketbook of Swoon* (Vagabond Press, 2014). In 2023, she took part in the Invisible Walls cross-cultural exchange between Australian and Korean poets.

Catherine Vidler grew up in Newcastle, studied in Sydney, and then lived and worked in the US and New Zealand for several years before returning to Sydney in 2004. Her poetry has been widely published in Australia, New Zealand, the US, the UK and elsewhere.

Anders Villani is the author of two poetry collections, *Aril Wire* (Five Islands Press, 2018) and *Totality* (Recent Work Press, 2022). He is the assistant poetry editor of *Australian Book Review*.

Dženana Vucic is a Bosnian-Australian writer currently based in Berlin. Her essays and poetry have been published in *Overland*, *Meanjin*, *Kill Your Darlings*, *Australian Poetry Journal*, *Cordite* and others. She has been awarded a 2022 Marten Bequest and the 2022 Peter Blazey Fellowship to work on an autotheoretical novel.

Corey Wakeling is a writer, translator, and scholar living in Tokyo, working as an associate professor of English literature at Aoyama Gakuin University. He was born in Lancashire in the UK, grew up in Perth, and undertook postgraduate studies in Melbourne. He was granted a PhD in English and Theatre Studies from the University of Melbourne in 2013. Corey's most recent book of poems is *Uncle of Cats* (Cordite, 2024).

Anne Walsh is a poet and a story writer. She has been shortlisted twice for both the Newcastle Poetry Prize and the ACU Prize for literature. Her work has been widely published in print and online in Australia and in the U.S. Her two poetry collections are *I Love Like a Drunk Does* published by Ginninderra Press in 2009 and *Intact*, published by Flying Islands Books in 2017. Recently, at the invitation of American actor Tituss Burgess, she read her work as part of Carnegie Hall's inaugural live online concert.

Jen Webb lives on Ngunnawal country in Canberra, where she is Distinguished Professor of Creative Practice at the University of Canberra. Author or editor of 30 scholarly volumes, she has also published 20 poetry collections and artist books, and is co-editor of the bilingual (Mandarin/English) anthology *Open Windows: Contemporary Australian Poetry*, and the literary journal *Meniscus*. Her most recent poetry collections are *Flight Mode* (with Shé Hawke, 2020) and *The Daily News* (Recent Work Press, 2024).

Jessica L. Wilkinson has published three poetic biographies, most recently *Music Made Visible: A Biography of George Balanchine* (Vagabond, 2019). Jessica is the founding editor of *Rabbit: a journal for nonfiction poetry*—which will soon release its 40th issue—and the offshoot Rabbit Poets Series of single-author collections by emerging Australian poets. She co-edited the anthologies *Contemporary Australian Feminist Poetry* (2016) and *Memory Book: Portraits of Older Australians in Poetry and Watercolours* (2021). She teaches Creative Writing at RMIT University, Melbourne.

Panda Wong is a poet living on unceded Wurundjeri country. Working across sound, performance, moving image and digital spaces, her work explores the more-than-human world, grief as prayer and ritual, communion with the dead and language's processes of rupture and reunion. Collaboration and friendship are core to her practice. In 2022, she published her debut chapbook *angel wings dumpster fire*, which was shortly followed by her first poetry EP *salmon cannon me into the abyss*. She also co-edited *Best of Australian Poems 2023*.

Grace Yee is the author of *Chinese Fish* (Giramondo Publishing), winner of the Victorian Prize for Literature, the Victorian Premier's Literary Award for Poetry, and the Mary and Peter Biggs Award for Poetry at the Ockham New Zealand Book Awards, in 2024. Her poetry has been widely published and anthologised across Australia and internationally, and has been awarded the Peter Steele Poetry Award, the Patricia Hackett Prize, and a Creative Fellowship at the State Library Victoria. Grace lives in Melbourne, on Wurundjeri land.

Ouyang Yu is an award-winning poet and novelist. His first novel, *The Eastern Slope Chronicle*, won the 2004 South Australian Festival Award for Innovation in Writing. His third novel, *The English Class*, won the 2011 NSW Premier's Award, and his 14th collection of poetry, *Terminally Poetic* (2020), won the Judith Wright Calanthe Award for a Poetry Book in the 2021 Queensland Literary Awards. He was shortlisted for the Writer's Prize in the 2021 Melbourne Prize for Literature and won the Fellowship from Creative Australia in late 2021 for writing a documentary novel, now complete in three volumes. And his eighth novel, *All the Rivers Run South*, was published in December 2023 by Puncher & Wattmann, which is also publishing his ninth novel, *The Sun at Eight or Nine*, in 2024, and his first collection of short stories, *The White Cockatoo Flowers*, is out in early 2024 with Transit Lounge Publishing.

Born in Beijing, **Gavin Yuan Gao** is a poet and translator based in Meanjin (Brisbane). Their debut poetry collection, *At the Altar of Touch* (UQP 2022), won the 2020 Arts Queensland Thomas Shapcott Poetry Prize, the 2023 Victorian Premier's Poetry Prize, and the 2023 Prime Minister's Literary Award for Poetry.

Guest Editors

Kate Lilley is the author of three books of poetry—most recently *Tilt* (Vagabond 2018), winner of the Victorian Premier's Award for Poetry—and many essays. She has edited two collections, *Margaret Cavendish: The Blazing World and Other Writings* (Penguin Classics) and *Dorothy Hewett: Selected Poems* (UWAP). She was a member of the English Department at the University of Sydney 1990–2021 where she is now an Honorary Associate Professor.

Shastra Deo was born in Fiji, raised in Melbourne, and lives in Brisbane. Her first book, *The Agonist* (UQP 2017), won the 2016 Arts Queensland Thomas Shapcott Poetry Prize and the 2018 Australian Literature Society Gold Medal. Her second book, *The Exclusion Zone*, was published by University of Queensland Press in 2023.

Acknowledgements and Publication Details

Chris Andrews' 'Under Fang' appeared in *The Weekend Australian*, 26–27 August 2023.

Manisha Anjali's extracted pages appear in the book-length poem, *Naag Mountain*, by Manisha Anjali (Giramondo, April 2024).

Stuart Barnes' 'The record player' appeared in *Island*, August 2023.

Ender Başkan's 'our neighbours poem' appeared in *Overland* online, 3/11/2023.

Damien Becker's 'Atrophy' was commissioned by *Regional Review* (ed. Claire Albrecht) to be published in August 2024.

Judith Beveridge's 'Dead Possum' appeared in *Live Encounters Poetry & Writing Special Australian Edition*, August 2023.

Ken Bolton's 'And John, A Note to You' was unpublished but written during the *BoAP 2024* time frame. It appeared in *No Placebos* in September 2024.

joanne burns's 'cataloggia' appeared in *Mascara* 29.

Pascalle Burton's 'iron filings (after Liliane Lijn's *Solar Cutting*)' was created as part of *Author Unknown*, the collaborative writing project by David Stavanger and Pascalle Burton, and was first published by Red Room Poetry. It incorporates the following found texts provided to Pascalle by Liliane Lijn: Paul Davies' 2018 article 'History's most successful mathematical prediction' in *Cosmos* magazine, Canaccord Genuity Wealth Management's *Intelligent Investing*, February 2022, and Chapters 26–30 of Janson's *History of Art: The Western Tradition*.

Luoyang Chen's 'No Cinematic Act Could Counterfeit' appeared in *Cordite Poetry Review*, September 2023.

Eileen Chong's 'The Mechanisms of Doorknobs' appeared in *Liminal Magazine: Synthesis* on 8 November 2023 at https://www.liminalmag.com/synthesis/eileen-chong

Emilie Collyer's 'Lateral ambling gait' was runner-up in the 2024 Gwen Harwood Poetry Prize and appeared in *Island* 170, March 2024.

Stuart Cooke's poem is part of the complete, 13-page version of 'Repetend' which was published in *Golden Handcuffs Review* (USA, July 2024); a 6-page extract was published in *The Chicago Review* (USA, February 2024).

Amy Crutchfield's 'Overheated' was published in *Overland* 251, Winter 2023.

Cath Drake's 'Snow Burial' was longlisted by the University of Canberra's Vice Chancellor's International Poetry Prize in 2023 and included in their anthology *Being* in 2024.

Dave Drayton's 'Centocartography: Heathcote' was published in *Rabbit* 39: Mutiny.

Willo Drummond's 'Learning to use a drill at forty-three' was first published in *Island* 168, July 2023.

Michelle D'Souza's 'Birthday Letter' appeared in *Plumwood Mountain, Volume 11, no. 1*, April 2024, 'Queering Ecopoet(h)ics' (Eds. Stuart Barnes and Dr Willo Drummond).

Michael Farrell's 'Wrong Forest' appeared in *Blackbox Manifold* 31, January 2024.

Jo Gardiner's 'A Country Childhood' appeared in *The Crossing: Newcastle Poetry Prize Anthology*, Hunter Writers Centre, November 2023.

Angela Gardner's 'A Passage Through' appeared in *Anthropocene*, May 2024.

Jake Goetz's 'By a drowned valley estuary: three tracings' was shortlisted for the University of Sydney's David Harold Tribe Poetry Prize (2023) and was published in *Overland* 253, Summer 2023.

Rory Green's 'The time traveler promises it all' appeared in *Cordite Poetry Review: TREAT*, May 2024.

Kerry Greer's 'Three Days and Six Years' was published in *Island* 170, as part of being shortlisted for the 2024 Gwen Harwood Poetry Prize.

Ashley Haywood's 'The Tableland Hour' appeared in *Polyp*, by Ashley Haywood (Vagabond Press, 2024).

Dan Hogan's 'Workarounds' won the 2024 Peter Porter Poetry Prize and was published in *Australian Book Review*, no. 461.

L K Holt's 'Describe the Singularity in the Style of Emily Dickinson' was first published in *Three Books*, by L K Holt (Vagabond Press, 2024).

Duncan Hose's 'The Lumpen Aristocrats (Paris)' appeared in *No Placebos* no. 7 (Donnithorne Street Press 2024), and *The Lumpen Aristocrats* (now orries press, 2024).

Andy Jackson's 'You speak clouds' appeared in *The Marrow* (Issue 1), July 2024.

Anna Jacobson's 'Memory Curls' was published in *Anxious in a Sweet Store*, by Anna Jacobson (Upswell, 2023).

Hannah Jenkins's forest void' was published in *The HTML Review*, March 2024. You can access the work here: https://thehtml.review/03/forest-void/ and you can read more about this publication here: https://thehtml.review/about

Jill Jones' 'Thinking in the Heat Wave About Clothes, Coins, Yearning, Flying Foxes and What I Cannot Escape' was first published in *Modron Magazine*, Earth Day 2024 Feature, 22 April 2024 (UK).

Georgia/George Kartas' and **Madison Griffith**'s 'Causality' was first published in issue 4 of *Crawlspace*, 2024 (https://crawlspace.cool/). 'The Empress' is one of 22 image-and-text poems in the digital tarot work.

Louis Klee's 'Landscape Poets' was written and previously unpublished within the *BoAP 2024* timeframe. It appeared in their chapbook *Poets and their Enemies* (Slow Loris) subsequently.

Jeanine Leane's '2020 Vision' appeared in *Gawimarra: Gathering*, by Jeanine Leane (UQP, January 2024).

Felicity Plunkett's 'Tender' appeared in *Plumwood Mountain, Volume 11*, no. 1, April 2024, 'Queering Ecopoet(h)ics' (Eds. Stuart Barnes and Dr Willo Drummond).

Julie Manning's 'Evening on the River' appeared in *Australian Book Review*, July 2024.

Shey Marque's 'Synaesthesia through Binoculars' was commissioned and first published in *Westerly Online: djinda*, November 2023.

Jini Maxwell's 'Where it Lives' appeared in *Overland* 252, Spring, 2023.

Chloe Mayne's 'larapuna' appeared in *Overland* 254. It also placed third in the Judith Wright Poetry Prize this year.

Scott-Patrick Mitchell's 'I try to talk to gay men on first dates about Perth Canyon and Deep Time but they don't care' appeared in *Plumwood Mountain*, Vol. 11, no. 1, April 2024, 'Queering Ecopoet(h)ics' (Eds. Stuart Barnes and Dr Willo Drummond).

Roslyn Orlando's poem appeared in the book-length poem, *Ekhō*, by Roslyn Orlando (Upswell, January 2024).

Esther Ottaway's 'On whether I subscribe to my name' appeared in *The Suburban Review*, issue 31: Subscribe, September 2023.

Claire Potter's 'Black Market' appeared in *Australian Book Review*, June 2024.

Stephanie Powell's 'Touch free wash' appeared in *Island* 169, November 2023.

Nadia Rhook's 'after the borders open I'm flying to home with poems' was first published in the anthology, *Poetry of Home*, Liquid Amber Press Poetry Prize, November 2023.

Autumn Royal's 'Reception Theory or How to Sit in an Office Chair' appeared in *Going Down Swinging*, 29 September 2023.

Sara M Saleh's 'Unholy Verses' appeared in *The Flirtation of Girls/Ghazal el-Banat*, by Sara M Saleh (UQP, November 2023).

Omar Sakr's 'Bluey in the Genocide' is part of *The Nightmare Sequence*.

Ali Jane Smith's 'Still Life appeared in Brown' appeared in the *Chroma* anthology published by South Coast Writers Centre, June 2024.

Hazel Smith's 'Unbalancing' has been published in audio form on *Duelling* (CD by austraLYSIS, Earshift, 2024).

Thom Sullivan's 'Phalaris / Perennial' appeared in *Jacaranda Journal*, Edition 10.2 Summer, 2024.

Munira Tabassum Ahmed's 'The Boy Who Turned Into Butter' was published in *The Marrow International Poetry* (Issue 1).

Catherine Vidler's 'abc poem' appeared in *The Selected Visual Poems of Catherine Vidler* (Stale Objects dePress, November 2023).

Anders Villani's 'Calm Voice' appeared in *Australian Book Review* no. 463, April 2024.

Dženana Vucic's 'my father sits in a room alone' was shortlisted for the Newcastle Poetry Prize and published in *The Crossing: Newcastle Poetry Prize Anthology 2023*.

Jen Webb's 'Voice of America Shortwave Radio Towers Demolished' appeared in *Remnant* (Ed. C Atherton, Spineless Wonders, Strawberry Hills, 2024).

Jessica L. Wilkinson's 'Madeleine' was first published by the Red Room Company, December 2023.

Panda Wong's 'pork lullaby' appeared in a version which was shortlisted in the *Overland* Judith Wright Poetry Prize 2023 and was published in *Overland* (online).

Grace Yee's 'how to launch a poem' appeared in *Griffith Review* 85, July 2024.

Gavin Yuan Gao's 'Itinerant' was published in *Australian Book Review*, August 2024.

www.ingramcontent.com/pod-product-compliance
Lightning Source LLC
Chambersburg PA
CBHW030109170426
43198CB00009B/545